MARE MORTUUM, SALSUM sive SALIS, LACUS ASPHALTITIS

Olim vallis Salinarum, prædicatæ fœcunditatis & a
Post autem Sodoma eversa, mutata est in illan
qua hodie conspicitur. Divinæ ultionis admiranda

rhæi
Mephaath

Bamoth vallis
Abarim mons
Abyla Sisanÿ
Nebo
Nain
Beth. Peon
Callirrhoe
Mons Pisga
M. Nebo
Macherunta
Alexandria
abarim
Sittim
Bethabara
natha
Dooch
Cyprum.
Galgala
Hetæi
Fons Helisei
ophnæ
Aphara
Iherico
Adonim
IUDAEA
chia
Scharm
Tribus
Desertum Adomin
Bethauen
Hay
Mijchmas
Terra rosa
Fons Solis
Ennon
Bethel
Rimo m.
Lapis Behon
Gethsemani
Luza
Benjamin
Berphage
Montes Ephraim
Bahurim
Astaroth
Olivarum mons
Bethania
Napolosa
Rama
Anototh
Bethsura
Fons Iacob.
Ceslon
Gabaan
Bethlehem
hem
Bira, Ca-
phira
Satilis
Sion m.
Jdoe fons
Mons Ga-
rizim
Gazer
Bethoron su-
perior
Rama Silo
Hierusalem
Templu Iovis
Mons
Ebal
Macedo
Bethoron inferior
Socoth
Iebusæi.
Iuda
Labana
Lemna
Beth Da-
gon
Beroth
Emaus Nico-
polis
S. Phi-
lippi
Montana Iu-
dea.
Asan
Ether
Baula
Sophin
Eblon
Bethsemus
Azecha
Cariath Iarim
Botri Raphaim
Bala
Thamna
Lachis
Sarid
Arecho
Bethoron
Pontana
Saba
Tebbon
Beth Nobe vel
Bethnopolis
Eglom
Modin
Scirona
Chens
Sepulch. Machab.
Saurona
Lidda, vel
Diospolis
Cessalon
Ierimoth
Senir mons
Betsames
Geth, Gibelim.
Eluzeropolis
Gabathon
Rhainathaim
Rhama, &
Rhamula
Saron M.
Famnia Iudeoru portus
Dan
Caphar
Azotys, sive
Assod
Joppe n.
Iaffu
Castrum Beroaldi
Acaron
PHILIS:

Adama
Sodoma
Gomorra

Zegor
Engadi mons
Massada
Monast. S Ioan.
Vallis benedictio: nis
Quarentana mons
Bethabara
Herodium
S. Saba
Medyn
Coena
Bethulia castrum
Tecua
Esthemoa
Sachak
Vallis Iosaphat
Ader
Amam
Capella Nicolai
Sepulchru
Rachel
Bezeth
Sepulchru Beth
Tribus Iuda
Goliath m.
Kabzeel
Rama
Arab
Iuda
Bethzacha
Chebbon
Icblon
Vallis Mambre
Irsaines
Thimna
Nair
Adassa
Esiaol
Adollm

Desertum Maon
Carmelus Mons
Zyph
Loche
Asan Santainar
Ain Bedhenim
Sinæi
Maon
Hadassa
Loth
Gilo
Gederothaim
Gedera
Carmel
Thamna
Dabyr
Cariath Sephar
Enaim
Gerar
Enachim
Sophor cast.
Hebron, Cariath
Arba
Ceila
Gibilena
Tribus Simeon
Bersabe
Betgebrim
Carnob. S. Ioas
Herma
Bethlebaoth
Siccleg
Castellum Abrahæ
Mola
S. Samuel
Helrholad
Arma
Bethim huboth
Taph
Asersual
Bala
Gaza

IDUMAEA SU
IDUM
Sacr Torrens
Ascalon
thijm
Angaris mons

IN THE FOOTSTEPS OF JESUS

December 25, 1979

Merry Christmass

To Jean & Bob

Love, your Godson
John

IN THE FOOTSTEPS OF JESUS

 LEON AMIEL
PUBLISHER

WOLFGANG E. PAX

PHOTOGRAPHY BY DAVID HARRIS

EDITED BY MORDECAI RAANAN

DESIGNED BY PAUL KOR

Copyright © 1970, 1975 by NATEEV-printing & publishing enterprises ltd.
P.O.Box 6048, Tel-Aviv, Israel

De-Luxe Editions:

First Printing, October 1970
Second Printing, March 1971
Third Printing, December 1971
Fourth Printing, August 1972
Fifth Printing, July 1973
Sixth Printing, December 1973
Seventh Printing, July 1974
Eighth Printing, December 1974
Ninth Printing, August 1976
Tenth Printing, May 1976
Eleventh Printing, January 1977

Paper-Back Edition:
First Printing, 1973
Second Printing, October 1974
Third Printing, August 1976
Fourth Printing, September 1976

Published in:

Israel, by Nateev and Steimatzky, Tel-Aviv
United States of America, by Leon Amiel Publisher
Switzerland, by Walter Verlag, Olten und Freiburg im Breisgau
France, by Edition Arthaud, Paris et Grenoble
Italy, by Coines Edizioni spa, Roma
Brazil, by Bloch Editores, Rio de Janeiro
Mexico, by Editorial Menorah, Mexico D.F.

ISBN 0-8148-0630-9
Library of Congress catalog card number: 74-19868

Printed and Bound in Israel by Peli Printing Works, Ltd. Givatayim.

Why compose yet another "Life of Christ?" The answer is, of course, twofold. The subject itself is like a prism which shows innumerable, different facets of a character which was more than human. Secondly, every serious student of Christian beginnings has something to contribute when he writes a new book, providing insights and explanations which will interest and inspire. A third reason, in our own time, is that such writing can be highly illustrated by another near-perfect medium of communication, namely, modern photography, and this has been skilfully utilized in the present volume. The author is completely competent, a specialist in the biblical disciplines. He is fully conscious of the problems involved in trying to retrace Jesus' story. He is aware that, by reason of his very sources, there cannot be question of a history in the modern sense of the term: a written description of past events together with an analysis of their meaning, interconnection and unity, an examination based on philosophical principles. The individual evangelists did not attempt this but focused their attention on the personality of Jesus regarded as Lord. Each saw him through different eyes, for various audiences, always finding new traits yet unable to portray him fully once and for all. It is in this sense of Christian religious history that the present volume has been set forth.

However, the author has added another dimension. Resident in the Holy Land for many years, he is a keen observer of the Oriental ways of life. A description of these, rightly understood, can throw fresh light on the Gospel record, bringing life, movement and color to what must otherwise remain something reflected as in a mirror. It is this new dimension which adds charm to the present work.

For instance, the query as to how Jesus actually looked can be answered by taking note of modern Oriental features: dark eyes, deep and compassionate and sensitive to atmosphere. It is this which gives importance to the very act of "looking" in the Bible. Jesus' garments must have been the traditional ones: a sleeveless gown, covered by another, completed by sandals and staff. The head-covering would have been a white cloth similar to the Arab KEFFIYEH of today, held in place by a cord. Many inhabitants of the Holy Land today are conversant with two or more languages. Since Jesus could speak to foreigners like Pilate without an interpreter he would have known some Greek as well as Aramaic and Hebrew. His boyhood would have been like that of others in the lush Galilee of old. He would have observed the activity of the world about him: the sower, the harvester, the vintner. He would have known the secrets of the fig tree, the briar, the sycamore, the tiny mustard seed. He would have seen the ways of birds building their nests, of foxes hiding in their shelters. All this and more was to come to life later in his parables. Above all, he observed people in all their various ways of life, with all their different traits.

The manner of his formal religious education can also be illustrated: Jewish prayers in the home, scripture readings, synagogue services, all contributing to that fund of learning which the boy Jesus displayed before Jerusalem's own teachers in their very Temple. In this he was truly a BAR MITZVAH, a genuine heir of the Old Testament traditions.

Thus, the author of the present book shows himself familiar with a host of detail underlying the New Testament texts. With restrained artistry, he throws light on one or other episode which the reader has never, perhaps, understood fully before. This is especially so when he penetrates outward events and refers to traits of Oriental psychology itself.

Rapid changes of mood, for instance, can be thus explained. Even amidst his triumphal entry into Jerusalem Jesus could break down and weep over the future fate of the city. Complementary to this constant reference in the text to Jewish life as revived in the Holy Land at present is the rich photography of actual events, situations and shrines. The book is by far the most profusely illustrated of its kind in the sense that nearly all the pictures are in color. Thus, the reader can, on the one hand, enjoy the beauty of Galilee in springtime: the rich vegetation of the farmlands, the green of the vines, the gold of the harvest and, as background, the calm blue of the incomparable Sea of Galilee. At the same time, he can study the detail of Christian monuments: the original color of mosaics, the detail of paintings, the grace of architectural lines. In some churches, interior photography is quite difficult. In this respect, the illustrations in this book are highly successful.

There are other features of the work which can be admired, notably the author's close knowledge of New Testament chronology, his sense of the pressures brought to bear on Jesus throughout his public ministry, the manner of his trial and death. However, it is the overall sense of reverence which appeals, especially in an age when it has become fashionable to dismiss so much. Perhaps, by this more than by any other single element, the author has helped remind us of the permanence of the Gospel story. Having retraced the footsteps of Jesus once more, Christians will realize that his life has fundamental meaning still, that Jesus of Nazareth still dwells amongst us "wherever his ministry is recalled and his word preached."

Gerard Bushell, O.F.M.

Throughout the world there are many holy places frequented by people on pilgrimage in order to draw closer to God. However, there is really only *one* Holy Land, and that is, in Hebrew usage, Eretz Israel. Here God has repeatedly revealed himself and shown mankind how to live according to his commandments. Why this should have been the Chosen Land is his secret which none may fathom. Seen geographically and historically, The Holy Land is a gateway between two continents and that means movement, unrest. Perhaps God wishes to symbolize to mankind that, concealed, he is nevertheless master of all life, the focal point of light and rest in the midst of the confusion of time and in spite of all the natural difficulties which mankind does not know how overcome. Looked at this way, the Holy Land becomes for us all both an example and a parable, and the call to peace—*Shalom, Pax Tecum*—a vital appeal out of the distant past which cannot be ignored even today.

We are on the Mount of Olives, looking over the city of Jerusalem, which has been destroyed often and has always been rebuilt; it seems to be petrified and yet its narrow streets and alleys are brimming over with life. This is the City of David, once the political center of the Jewish people; but above all it has been and remains its religious center. The prophet Ezekiel called it "the center of the earth." The Psalmist celebrates it in song as the mother of mankind (87:5) and Isaiah speaks of the royal feast which the Lord will prepare for his people on Mount Zion when the Messiah comes, and "the Lord God will wipe away tears from all faces" (25:8).

Through the still air we can hear the sound of the bells from the Holy Sepulchre, from Gethsemane, and from the Dormition Abbey. It is as if their harmonious sounds were echoing the final words spoken on earth by Jesus Christ: "And lo, I am with you always, to the close of the age" (Matthew 28:20). It is very mysterious that through the person of Jesus, Eretz Israel was chosen a second time to be the setting in which God made himself manifest. The country cannot be imagined without him, his life reached its climax in Jerusalem. The evangelist Luke, who was a stranger born elsewhere and of another people, realized

"...the angel Gabriel was sent from God to a city of Galilee named Nazareth"

(Luke 1:26)

Nazareth is Christianity's most holy town. Climbing the foothills of lower Galilee, it has been called "Watchtower." Nestling in its own valley, it has been known also as the "Flower of Galilee". Here Christianity began, nearly two thousand years ago.

earlier and more clearly than the other evangelists that Jerusalem was to be the final goal of Jesus. His entry into the Holy City on Palm Sunday is described by Luke as if it were the beginning of the time of the Messiah; the multitude rejoices: "Blessed is the King who comes in the name of the Lord! Peace in heaven and glory in the highest!" (Luke 19:38).

THE LIFE OF JESUS

It is difficult, if not actually impossible, to write about the earthly existence of Jesus of Nazareth. We are much better informed about his contemporaries, the Roman Emperors Augustus and Tiberius, as well as about King Herod. Certainly we have some reliable sources. Apart from brief references in extrabiblical literature which testify to the existence of Jesus, the most important material is provided by the Gospels. But their writers were not concerned with producing a historical biography in the modern manner. They took as their focus the personality of the Lord.

As is sometimes the case when one is dealing with a beloved person, his words and deeds

11

The Church of the Annunciation (right), completed in 1969, is most modern in style. The massive block of its masonry symbolizes permanence, even eternity. Its dome opens like a flower over one of Christianity's most sacred spots, a cave (left), once part of a dwelling where, tradition says, Mary received heavenly news that she was to be Christ's mother.

were indelibly impressed upon the memories of the writers of the Gospels. Each of the evangelists sees Jesus with different eyes. They regard his figure, so to speak, from all sides, continually discovering new traits and yet unable to describe him once and for all. The Gospels which have been handed down to us accumulated slowly in the course of the first century after Christ: stories of what Jesus did and what he said, based on the accounts of eyewitnesses, were told in the families and collected according to certain theological points of view, to be used as liturgy, as teaching material, and as catechism. The presentation of the religious problems was naturally influenced by the Jewish way of thought, while the language used was Greek of the Diaspora.

The life of Jesus is closely woven into the history of Palestine. The scenes of his life are well known to us through the excavations of the last few decades. Archaeology provides the proof that the good tidings were not derived from subjective experiences but closely related to the actual events of the world, and that the evangelists, therefore, are reporting true facts.

Certainly we have to be aware that archaeology has its limitations. There is no place bearing a sign, such as we would put up today, with the inscription: HERE DWELT JESUS OF NAZARETH. As the result of the effects of the climate, earthquakes, and the destruction of wars, the appearance of many of the places has changed in the course of the centuries. And what has been even more decisive: soon after Jesus died, the Holy Land was occupied by the Romans, and Jews and Christians were expelled, especially from Jerusalem. Christianity was not officially recognized by the state until 300 years later, under the Emperor Constantine. In the fifth to seventh centuries after Jesus, Christian life blossomed forth. Many pilgrims came from all parts of the known world to visit the holy places, and many churches were built. With few exceptions, the earliest archaeological finds of interest to us here date from this period. But at least some of them are based on the ancient traditions and so recall for us the life of Jesus. Perhaps it is not so important that sometimes the actual events occurred in a different place. The numerous Byzantine churches which can be

12

O favored one, the Lord is with you!" *(Luke 1:28)*

found in the most remote corners of Samaria and Galilee bear witness to the response which the word of the Lord found in the hearts of the faithful. The host of pilgrims continues to this day. Each generation has paid its homage to the holy places by adding new buildings, from the Crusaders to builders today. Modern churches deliberately incorporate ancient remains uncovered by excavation as an effective way of expressing their close relationship to the originals.

The life of Jesus is made more real and immediate when it is visualized against the landscape which was its setting. Goethe said: "If you want to understand the poet you must visit his country." These words by the great German poet, with of course a little adaptation, are never more apt than when applied to the realm of the Bible. In the Middle East people live in the open air. Jesus preached not only in the synagogue but attracted crowds especially in the hills, in the fields, on the lake shore, and in the marketplace. He was receptive to the impressions the countryside made on him, and his parables reflect the reality of the realm of nature which to him was symbolic

of the supernatural. In October, after the first rains, the stony mountainsides suddenly become radiant with flowers, especially with red anemones. Automatically the question arises how such an abundance of fertility is possible in the midst of such dearth; this phenomenon of nature provides the background for the words of the Lord: "Consider the lilies of the field, how they grow; they neither toil nor spin; yet I tell you, even Solomon in all his glory was not arrayed like one of these" (Matthew 6:28—29).

The desert is huge and solitary, with its play of colors when the shadows grow long and the sand gleams a brilliant white, while the vaulted sky luminous with stars arches above it; only someone who has himself walked there can conceive of it as a place of salvation. It makes us realize how it came about that the Children of Israel received their religion during their sojourn in the desert, and why Jesus withdrew into the desert for forty days. But one must also be familiar with its danger: anyone who has himself been deceived in the white heat of a summer's day by a mirage in the Jordan Valley will realize how seriously the Lord must

15

have been tempted when the devil "showed him all the kingdoms of the world and the glory of them; and he said to him, 'All these I will give you, if you will fall down and worship me'" (Matthew 4:8—9). Anyone who has been refreshed, after a long journey, by a mouthful of water from a spring or a well will realize the depth of meaning contained in the image of "living water" which Jesus uses in his conversation with the woman of Samaria by Jacob's well (John 4:10).

But above all, Palestine is the land of light. Anyone who has seen the magnificent view of the sun rising or setting above the Holy City, or the solitary translucent clouds above the Mount of Olives, will have realized why light has played such an important part in religious thought. Isaiah already sang: "And nations shall come to your light, and kings to the brightness of your rising" (60:3). The Jewish community at Qumran by the Dead Sea believed the meaning of their life to be the struggle of the sons of light against the sons of darkness. Jesus, the supreme, says of himself: "I am the light of the world" (John 8:12).

This is a peopled landscape. Jesus felt very close to people; everyone who crossed his path was to him a brother, related to him. The Middle East is unchanging. One can still encounter the same types of people today. One of the most moving sights in the Old City of Jerusalem is the blind, who always go about in pairs. Jesus' disciples were annoyed by the innumerable children in the alleys and squares; but he called to them: Let the children come to me, and do not hinder them; for to such belongs the kingdom of heaven" (Matthew 19:14). Orthodox people strive to achieve their salvation by observing faithfully all the commandments; their environment today is similar to that in which Jesus disputed with them. Habits and customs have not changed much in outlying districts, especially in those which are inhabited mainly by Arabs and are bypassed by the usual tourist routes. Many couples still marry in the way which is described in the parable of the virgins; even today the bridegroom comes at nightfall with torches to the sound of music into the house of his bride (Matthew 25:1). Especially hospitality plays an important part in the life of Jesus and reaches its climax when we are invited to his

17

When Jesus walked through the market he must have known much the same atmosphere as today, the same merchandise (below), the same colors, the same smells. The Greek Catholic Church (right) by the market houses the ancient synagogue where Jesus is said to have gone to school.

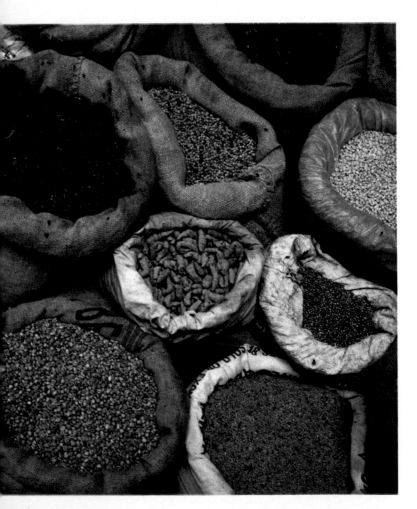

table; it is one of the virtues most highly regarded among the Bedouins.

THE ORIGIN

It is as if Pilate had issued an official document when he had the famous inscription put on the CROSS: JESUS OF NAZARETH THE KING OF THE JEWS. At that time, Jesus was a comparatively common name; on the Mount of Olives an ossuary has been found bearing the same name. One may assume that the mentioning of the hometown is intended to avoid confusion between people with similar names. And so the first disciples were called Nazarenes; the denomination "Christians" arose outside Palestine in the Syrian city of Antioch.

It is strange that Nazareth is not cited either in the Old Testament or in Talmudic literature. Flavius Josephus, who led the Jewish troops in Galilee against the Romans, mentioned the neighboring towns of Sepphoris, the former residence of Herod Antipas, and the even nearer Jotapata (Yodfat), which was conquered by Titus — but about Nazareth he is silent. It must, therefore, have been an unimportant little place, which makes it under-

standable that Nathanael asks John: "Can anything good come out of Nazareth?" (John 1:46).

There are geographical reasons for this. The ancient Via Maris, which linked Damascus with Gaza and Egypt, passed about six miles east of Mount Tabor to join, in the plain of Esdraelon, the highway which led from the Jordan to the Mediterranean. Today Nazareth is a center; its meaning to Christianity has provided it with significance. But because it lies in a valley, from which the surrounding hills rise like amphitheaters, it was bypassed by the traffic of ancient times. But it is a fact that part of the Carmel range and Galilee were already inhabited in the Stone Age, and the discovery of cave dwellings in the district confirm that the same may well be true of Nazareth. In the neighborhood of the Church of the Annunciation, not far from the spring, many grottoes and wine and olive presses have been found, and also silos and cisterns dating from Roman times. These prove that the district was inhabited during this period and that its population lived by agriculture. Small houses with flat roofs and grottoes cut out of

the rock to provide them with storerooms still exist today; they may well have filled the valley and covered the sides of the hills even at that time.

We are standing here on historic ground, even though in the history of the world at that time the place was of no importance and might by now well have been long forgotten. Because this is where Jesus lived, however, its name reverberates across the world to this day.

It was in Nazareth that an event took place which we can only approach with the greatest reverence. Luke, who abhorred all sensationalism, provides a plain report; it makes a profound impression precisely because of its simplicity—and it may well be based on Mary's original account: "In the sixth month the angel Gabriel was sent from God to a city of Galilee named Nazareth, to a virgin betrothed to a man whose name was Joseph, of the house of David; and the virgin's name was Mary. And he came to her and said, 'Hail, O favored one, the Lord is with you! But she was greatly troubled at the saying and considered in her mind what sort of greeting this might be. And the angel said to her, 'Do not be afraid,

Mary, for you have found favor with God. And behold, you will conceive in your womb and bear a son, and you shall call his name Jesus. He will be great and will be called the Son of the Most High; and the Lord God will give to him the throne of his father David, and he will reign over the house of Jacob for ever; and of his kingdom there will be no end.' And Mary said to the angel, 'How can this be, since I have no husband?' And the angel said to her, 'The Holy Spirit will come upon you, and the power of the Most High will over-shadow you; therefore the child to be born will be called holy, the Son of God. And behold, your kinswoman Elizabeth in her old age has also conceived a son; and this is the sixth month with her who was called barren. For with God nothing will be impossible.' And Mary said, 'Behold, I am the handmaid of the Lord; let it be to me according to your word.' And the angel departed from her" (Luke 1:26—38).

An angel, through whom the voice of God is speaking, greets a young Jewish woman about fifteen years old; she is already wedded to her husband Joseph but the nuptials have not yet been celebrated. Those who are familiar with the Middle East will know that the greeting itself is of the utmost importance; it may take many different forms and the subsequent conversation can achieve its purpose only if the correct form of address has been used. There is a greeting suitable for a chance encounter in the street, one to be used between men, one between women. The greeting exchanged between married people differs from that used between those who are unmarried; that used between parents and children is different again. How melodious is the sound of the word *shalom,* how well Mozart called the angel's greeting in his *Ave Maria!* "Hail, full of grace, the Lord is with you. Hail thou that art highly favored," is a single musical phrase: Mary, like some of the woman in the Old Testament, has been accorded God's grace; she has been called, she has been chosen. At the moment when the words are spoken she is already surrounded by God's peace and filled with joy. Mary is confused, because no one she knows has ever used such a greeting. The angel exclaims: "Do not be afraid, Mary." This phrase frequently accompanies supernatural

"In those days Mary arose and went with haste into the

Seeking further light on the mystery of the Annunciation, Mary hastened south into the hill country of Judah to the town of her kinswoman, Elizabeth. Tradition indentifies the settlement as Ein Karem, now a suburb of Jerusalem.

manifestations, reassuring the recipient of God's personal affection; he announces that she has been chosen to bear the Messiah and refers to Isaiah's ancient prophecy: "A young woman shall conceive and bear a son" (7:14). At the same time, the child's future importance is emphasized; God will grant him the throne of his ancestor David, as has been predicted: "And your house and your kingdom shall be made sure for ever before me; your throne shall be established forever" (2 Samuel 7:16).

Mary had been brought up strictly in the Jewish tradition and therefore has a great respect for marriage; this explains her question: "How can this be?" But God does not ask of her anything to which her conscience might object. The Holy Ghost, which means God's own creative power, will cast a shadow and settle upon her; we are reminded of the passage in Exodus 40:34 in which the cloud filled the tabernacle as a symbol of the presence of the glory of the Lord. In the Bible, such tidings are frequently confirmed by the granting of a sign; Mary is told about the pregnancy of her cousin Elizabeth, which had been kept a secret. Mary understands. Her answer, "Let it be to me according to your word," is her reply to the greeting, which the conversation has amplified and explained. To this day, an Arab will acknowledge a greeting by making a bow with his hand placed against his chest as an indication that he is willing to obey another's wish. Mary bows before God; she is used to filial obedience toward her father and knows that she had been taken possession of by God and that this will influence everything that will happen to her from now on: *Fiat voluntas tua!*

On the way from Haifa to Nazareth, as the road begins to descend into a valley, one is granted an indescribable view of the cupola of a new church, which looks as if it were suspended from the sky and about to settle on the sea of rooftops; one is reminded of John's saying: "And the Word became flesh and dwelt [literally: pitched the tent] among us" (John 1:14). From nearby, the church is almost too heavy and solid to express the tender and mysterious event of the Annunciation. The main entrance is artistically decorated with notable sculptures representing

hill country, to a city of Judah ... and greeted Elizabeth''

(Luke 1:39–40)

scenes from the Old and New Testaments. Within, one is surprised by the spaciousness: here one church has been built on top of another. Beneath the cupola, traces can be seen of the old Byzantine church, which was described by the pilgrim Anonymous of Piacenza (about A.D. 570): "The house of St. Mary is a basilica in which many miracles are performed by her garments." From this we may gather that Nazareth was at that time a frequent place of pilgrimage because it had been the place of the Annunciation. In the lower strata, archaeologists have discovered a pre-Byzantine synagogue building with the inscription XE MARIA. Even if the history of the grotto, which has become the center of worship today, is unclear, the discoveries show unequivocally that Nazareth has long been a place of reverence.

Today it is not possible to determine just where the meeting took place; it is also not important. The pilgrim Arkulf (about 670) reports that the church was built in the place where once stood the house which the archangel entered to speak to St. Mary. It is almost certain that the Annunciation took place in a small dwelling built of stone, which may soon afterward have been destroyed like any other house. The devout transferred their worship to one of the grottoes in the neighborhood; in Palestine grottoes are frequently associated with religious observances.

In one of the Gospels of the Apocrypha, which in the second century elaborated the sober accounts of the Holy Scriptures with legends, it is said of the Annunciation: "And Mary took the pitcher and went forth to fill it with water: and lo a voice saying: 'Hail, thou that are highly favored; the Lord is with thee: blessed art thou among women.' And she looked about her upon the right hand and upon the left, to see whence this voice should be: and being filled with trembling she went to her house and set down the pitcher and took the purple and sat down upon her seat and drew out the thread. And behold an angel of the Lord stood before her saying . . ." (Protevangelium of James 11:1).

Nazareth possesses one single spring which never runs dry; today its waters are channeled into a draw well, near which stands the Greek Orthodox Church of St. Gabriel. It is a charm-

Lord, and my spirit rejoices in God my Savior'" *(Luke 1:46–47)*

The courtyard of the Church of the Visitation, Ein Karem. The *Magnificat* is inscribed in forty-one languages on the plaques behind. In this song Mary rejoiced that she was to be the mother of the Lord.

ing picture when women, having filled their jugs, walk home balancing them on their heads. Mary must often have done likewise. This place, where women meet and gossip for a while, offers a typical Middle Eastern scene of daily life. The encounter might easily have taken place here. But the tradition is too recent to be given credence.

The mystery of the Incarnation explains why Jesus is frequently called the "Son of Mary." On occasion, accusations have been made against Mary. Even the Koran later came to her defense: "This was Jesus the Son of Mary: the word is truth" (Sura 19:35). Joseph accepted the miracle and took Mary as his wife. It was through him that Jesus became the "Son of David," as in ancient times questions of descent were determined only according to legal and not according to biological considerations. Since family tradition and a record of the generations play an important part in Judaism, the descent of Joseph from David may be accepted as historically true. He is one of those figures, so frequent especially among the Bedouin, who live in poverty but whose bearing and looks

> *"…(Elizabeth) exclaimed… 'why is this granted me that the mother of my Lord should come to me?'"*
>
> *(Luke 1:42–43)*

The mosaic on the facade of the Church of the Visitation shows Mary on her way from Nazareth to Elizabeth's home.

manifest a dignity that can derive only from a splendid past.

THE BIRTH

The birth of Christ, in about the year 7 B.C., is reported by Luke: "In those days a decree went out from Caesar Augustus that all the world should be enrolled. This was the first enrollment, when Quirinius was governor of Syria. And all went to be enrolled, each to his own city. And Joseph also went up from Galilee, from the city of Nazareth, to Judea, to the city of David, which is called Bethlehem, because he was of the house and lineage of David, to be enrolled with Mary, his betrothed, who was with child. And while they were there, the time came for her to be delivered. And she gave birth to her first born son and wrapped him in swaddling cloths and laid him in a manger, because there was no place for them in the inn" (2:1 — 7).

The text, introduced by historical comments, almost gives the impression of an official document, relating, as was customary at that time, a birth to its contemporary public events and in this way certifying it. From this we may draw the important conclusion that Jesus was indeed a real person. At the same time, it allows us to see the event—at first apparently so unimportant—against the background of world history. The Roman Emperor is mentioned, and this reminds us that from 63 B.C. Palestine belonged to the Roman Empire and was a part of the province of Syria although the Jews, who had been granted special privileges, were allowed to manage their own affairs. King Herod the Great had even succeeded in gaining the confidence of the Romans to such an extent that they made him a king, although he was not supported by the Jews and depended entirely upon Rome.

Augustus and Jesus—chance or design? The early Fathers already pondered the problem why these two great figures should have been contemporaries. Augustus was not just any sovereign, one of a number, but certainly the most important ruler of antiquity. After all the political and social upheavals which had preceded him, the world saw him as the personification of its hopes for peace, as its savior. The Roman poet Virgil, in one of his famous poems, predicted the birth of a boy, and the

27

"...henceforth all generations will call me blessed"

(Luke 1:48)

Frescos and mosaics make the
Church of the Visitation the
gayest in the Holy
Land. Behind the altar, Mary
is seen in glory, venerated
by angels, Doctors of the
Church and saintly folk of
Christian history.

Fates, who according to ancient belief provided human beings with their destiny, sang for him: "Turn, spindles turn, and let the grand centuries come." But the Pax Augusta was not confined to the realm of politics; it was intended to bring about peace all over the world and the regeneration of the cosmos. And so the ruler of the world becomes "the savior," he is called Augustus — the word means "worthy of reverence" (as a god).

Augustus himself once expressed the desire to be the creator of "the optimum state" and said that he would hope until his last breath that the foundations which he had laid would survive forever undisturbed. Many years after his death, the great Alexandrian Jew Philo called him "the supreme benefactor." Mankind in his time had nearly reached the stage of exterminating itself, and perhaps would have had it not been for the advent of this one man, the ruler Augustus. He was the hero who averted disaster, because he overcame the defects the Hellenic world shared with that of the barbarians. It was he who not merely loosened but burst the bonds which had constrained and oppressed mankind. It was he

who liberated the cities, made order of the chaos; he was the guardian of the peace who apportioned to everyone his due. Certainly, Augustus did the utmost he could under the circumstances of the times for the benefit of all peoples. But he was obliged to realize that a human being cannot achieve perfection. His hopes remained unfulfilled. Under his successors, the foundations which he laid crumbled, and in A.D. 70 Jerusalem was destroyed. His great counterpart is Jesus, whose kingdom is not of this world and who was able to say: "On this rock I will build my church, and the powers of death shall not prevail against it" (Matthew 16:18).

Augustus and Jesus were not contemporaries by chance; they were representatives of two different spiritual worlds. A well-known scholar of the New Testament, Ethelbert Stauffer, expressed it thus: "Augustus displayed the capabilities and the limitations of the most perfect specimen of *Homo imperiosus*. That is the meaning of his story for the destiny of man. That is why his extreme achievements illuminate the enormous problems and the tragedy of historic events. Some-

29

thing is wrong with the history of the world. Something has to be put right, something must happen. We are faced with the problem which made history progress from Augustus to Jesus."

The immediate cause of the journey of Mary and Joseph to Bethlehem was the census. The Romans had an excellent administration, and the assessment of taxes was one of its main functions. This was the real purpose of the occasion, not merely to count the people. This census took place at regular intervals, especially in the conquered provinces which were the most important sources of revenue for the state. Such a census could of course not be accomplished uniformly in the whole country on a certain day, but had to be regulated by local conditions. And so Quirinius, who was governor of Syria, ordered the census in his province. It was superintended by his delegate, which probably means by Herod himself.

An Egyptian papyrus from A.D. 104 contains an ordinance for such a census, which might apply equally well to the one we are concerned with: "Gaius Vibius Maximus, governor of Egypt, proclaims: As we are about to take a census it is necessary to order all those who are for any reason away from home to return to their own districts so that the census can be taken in the usual way." Married women also had to obey this ruling; their presence was required in order that the number of people in each family could be ascertained. The land owned had to be declared in the respective community so it could be evaluated and the taxes assessed accordingly. And therefore Joseph had to make the journey to Bethlehem, where he had come from and owned some property; it was the native place of the house of David.

Unlike Nazareth, Bethlehem is frequently mentioned in the Bible; it lies about five miles beyond Jerusalem in a range of hills. It is the setting of the charming story of Ruth, who gleaned barley in the fields and became the ancestress of David, who was born in this town. The prophet Micah proclaims the coming of one who will rule in the last days in mysterious words, which have always been interpreted as referring to Jesus: "But you, O Bethlehem Ephrathah, who are little to be among the clans of Judah, from you shall

"*But his mother said,... 'he shall be called John'*"

(Luke 1:60)

The pledge of Mary's future
motherhood was the birth of
John the Baptist to Zechariah,
the priest, and Elizabeth.
The traditional locality where
this occurred is the garden town
of Ein Karem, "Vineyard Spring."

come forth for me one who is to be ruler in Israel, whose origin is from of old, from ancient days" (5:2).

Bethlehem is sometimes pictured as an unknown village in the lifetime of Jesus; this is far from true. Quite close to it passed the main road from Jerusalem to Gaza, via Hebron, which was a well-known market town. The prophet Jeremiah mentioned a caravansary, or inn, which stood nearby in 587 B.C. and offered refugees a resting place; it is likely that there was a similar place there at a later date. Between three and four miles to the east lies the Herodium, an isolated hill visible from miles around, on which Herod built his palace. At the foot of it was a town which could be reached only via Bethlehem, so that much traffic passed through. The Herodium was also the center of administration for all the places south of Jerusalem. And this explains why there should have been no room at the inn, which was a typical Middle Eastern *khan:* a rectangular wall surrounding an open space with a well, where the animals were unharnessed and people rested on the ground. At night the door was firmly closed.

Typical of the district are its many natural caves, which have frequently been artificially enlarged. They serve Bedouin and animals as shelters even today. As a local man, Joseph must have been familiar with them, especially with those on the eastern slopes which are close to the pastures. In such a cave Jesus was born. The plain and simple account by Luke was written without ulterior motives and is almost certainly based on fact. A cave traditionally associated with the event became a place of worship and in the fourth century the Emperor Constantine erected above it a basilica with five naves, the oldest extant Christian church. Naturally, the cave has been somewhat altered during the course of the centuries, but in outline it preserves its original design. It consists, like most of these places, of two parts, one above the other. The upper one serves as a dwelling place for people and the lower one contains a manger intended for animals; it could be observed from above. It is certainly not spacious enough to have accommodated many animals. The ox and the ass shown in pictures painted during the Middle Ages are a theological embellishment.

"...Joseph also went up... to Judea, to the city of David, which is called Bethlehem... to be enrolled with Mary, his betrothed, who was with child" *(Luke 2:4–5)*

It is a pity that the walls have been lined with slabs of marble or covered with sheets of asbestos; but here and there the bare rock still shows, especially in the roof of the cave, and allows us to imagine how it may perhaps have looked once upon a time.

According to the Apocryphal Gospel of James, which graphically describes the life of the people, Mary's labor pains began on the road shortly before they reached Bethlehem, and so Joseph lifted her from the ass and carried her into a grotto. In order to preserve the memory of "Mary's Rest," Christians in the fifth century erected a church which no longer exists today.

The birth probably took place during the season after the early rains, when the soil is softened and rapidly sprouts a covering of green. In the fertile fields surrounding Bethlehem the shepherds were tending their flocks when an angel appeared through whom God's voice reached them: "'Behold, I bring you good news of a great joy which will come to all the people; for to you is born this day in the city of David a Savior, who is Christ the Lord'" (Luke 2:10—11).

Bethlehem enshrines the grotto-stable where Jesus was born. The Holy Family settled here after moving from Nazareth. Here Joseph was called upon to register them during a Roman census, possibly because he had property there, certainly because he was of the family of David and Bethlehem was David's town.

"O Bethlehem... from you shall come a ruler who will govern my people Israel"
(Matthew 2:6)

Bethlehem's skyline proclaims it sacred to many faiths. The towers, left to right, mark St. Catherine's Latin church, the Basilica of the Nativity (square tower, the Greek Orthodox Community; white cupola, the Armenian Orthodox Community), the main mosque, the Lutheran Church (in front), the Greek Catholic church.

Among the Bedouins, when a woman has given birth to a child, her female relatives will address similar words to her husband waiting outside the tent: "We bring you good news of a great joy, for to you is born this day . . ." The account in the Bible, therefore, describes the ancient habits and customs surrounding a birth in this country, and in its choice of words emphasizes the incarnation in an inimitable manner. Equally rooted in the old traditions is the angels' song of praise which follows; its structure derives from ancient Jewish liturgy and now, as "Gloria in excelsis Deo," it is part of the regular Christian Sunday morning service: "Glory to God in the highest, and on earth peace among men with whom he is pleased!" (Luke 2:14).

Already in the fourth century, a church was built in the Shepherds' Field, together with a convent that was one of the largest in the region of Bethlehem. Nearby are numerous cisterns and caves which were used by the shepherds. The modern chapel is a circular structure, receiving light only from above and so symbolizing the relationship between earth and sky. From there one has a magnificent

The Basilica of the Nativity,
like an ancient fortress, has
withstood the ravages of
time and war, standing intact
since the early sixth century.
The single, low entrance is
pictured on the left hand side.

view of the town, to which the shepherds went as soon as the angel had spoken to them. We are again confronted with simple popular custom, as the congratulations by friends and acquaintances occasioned by a birth follow traditional rites. These are still observed in the Holy Land today.

CONCERNING THE INFANCY OF JESUS

Luke reports two important events: "And at the end of eight days, when he was circumcised, he was called Jesus, the name given by the angel before he was conceived in the womb. And when the time came for their purification according to the law of Moses, they brought him up to Jerusalem to present him to the Lord (as it is written in the law of the Lord, 'Every male that opens the womb shall be called holy to the Lord') and to offer a sacrifice according to what is said in the law of the Lord, 'a pair of turtledoves, or two young pigeons'" (Luke 2:21–24).

These two cermonies are reported simply as facts and provide further proof that the Holy Family faithfully observed the Jewish traditions which have survived to this day. Circum-

cision, which is generally practiced in the Middle East, was endowed by the Israelites with a deep religious significance, as it was recognized as the outward sign of the covenant God had made with Abraham: "This is my covenant, which you shall keep, between me and you and your descendants after you: Every male among you shall be circumcised" (Genesis 17:10).

Especially after the dispersion, circumcision became the distinguishing mark of a Jew. Only the circumcised may take part in the celebration of Passover. His circumcision is the occasion when the child receives his name; the oldest son is usually named after his grandfather. This was the general custom and explains why people were surprised when the mother of John the Baptist insisted that her son should be named John according to the angel's instruction: "And they said to her, 'None of your kindred is called by this name'" (Luke 1:61).

And Jesus also received the name which God had chosen for him.

Furthermore, according to the law, a woman who had given birth to a boy was considered unclean for forty days, which meant that she was not allowed to leave the house or to touch any holy object. At the end of this period she had to journey to Jerusalem to be pronounced clean by the high priest on duty at the Gate of Nicanor, which led to the temple; poor people had to sacrifice a pair of turtledoves, and the rich in addition a year-old lamb. Moreover, the firstborn was consecrated to the service of God, which was described as being "presented at the temple." But as the official servants of the religion were the Levites, the boy was ransomed, which meant the payment of five holy shekels either to the priests in the temple or to any other priest in the land. Luke specifically omits any mention of this payment of ransom, which for him had a symbolical significance, because in fact Jesus consecrated the whole of his existence to his father in heaven.

On this occasion, the Holy Family met an old man called Simeon in the temple, who exclaimed enthusiastically: "'Lord, now lettest thou thy servant depart in peace, according to thy word; for mine eyes have seen thy salvation which thou hast prepared in the presence of all peoples, a light for revelation to the Gentiles, and for glory to thy people Israel'" (Luke 2:29—32). And they also met an old woman called Anna, who praised God and gave thanks to him when she saw the child. It ought to be remembered that in the Middle East old people are held in especially high esteem, because they have gathered much wisdom and may realize things which are hidden from others. Anna is called a prophetess; the word is not used to indicate a profession but as an epithet due to an old woman who is dignified and devout and has always been faithful to God.

For reasons which we lack the information to understand, the Holy Family did not immediately return to Nazareth but remained for a certain time in Bethlehem and seems to have moved into a small stone dwelling; we do not know whether it was built by Joseph himself or belonged to one of his relatives. Today no trace of it remains.

One further aspect of the infant's early life may perhaps be emphasized: in the Middle East, much attention is paid to the suckling of babies. There is an Arabic saying: "The milk

Christ, Mary and John the Baptist
are represented in a medieval fresco
which decorates the Chapel of the
Tower in the Basilica of the Nativity.

will act on the character; a boy who has had plenty of mother's milk has a strong character, his head is full with his mother's milk." Mothers frequently nurse their children for two or three years. After Hannah had given birth to Samuel, she no longer went to the temple with her husband but remained at home, explaining: "'As soon as the child is weaned, I will bring him, that he may appear in the presence of the Lord, and abide there forever.' And when she had weaned him, she took him up with her . . . and she brought him to the house of the Lord at Shiloh; and the child was young" (1 Samuel 1:22, 24). The child must have been between three and four years old, because "the boy ministered to the Lord, in the presence of Eli the priest" (1 Samuel 2:11). Doubtlessly, his mother nursed him for such a long time in order to give him the strength to become a priest.

Not far from the Basilica of the Nativity in Bethlehem is the so-called Milk Grotto. According to legend, when Mary was nursing her child a few drops of milk fell on the rocks and turned them white. Already in the seventh century, "Mary's Milk" is mentioned as a

Steps to the right lead down to the
Manger in the Grotto of the Nativity. The
altar (right) commemorates the visit
of the Wise Men who adored the child Jesus.

"...she gave birth to her first-born son... laid him in a

The silver star marks the spot where
the Nativity is said to have occurred. The
fifteen lamps which surround it, were
donated by various Christian communities.

manger, because there was no place... in the inn" (Luke 2:7)

Floor mosaics took the place of carpets in early Christian Churches. This fifth-century design in Bethlehem's basilica reflects the agricultural interests of the faithful: apples, grapes and pomegranates.

relic of which this grotto is the only true source. Throughout the centuries, pilgrims have taken small pieces, as the chalk is said to possess miraculous powers. Even today, many Christians and Moslems come to this grotto, say a prayer, and take away a piece of the soft rock, which they grind to dust and mix with the food of nursing mothers to encourage the flow of their milk. Although this story is not of biblical origin, it reflects popular opinion and allows us to imagine Mary's concern for her child.

The famous story of the wise men from the East also belongs to this period: "Now when Jesus was born in Bethlehem of Judea in the days of Herod the king, behold, wise men from the East came to Jerusalem, saying, 'Where is he who has been born king of the Jews? For we have seen his star in the East, and have come to worship him.' When Herod the king heard this, he was troubled, and all Jerusalem with him" (Matthew 2:1—3). He questioned the chief priests and the scribes of the people as to where the Messiah might have been born, and received the answer: in Bethlehem.

So the king sent the wise men there, charging them to report to him what they might find: "When they had heard the king they went their way; and lo, the star which they had seen in the East went before them, till it came to rest over the place where the child was. When they saw the star, they rejoiced exceedingly with great joy; and going into the house they saw the child with Mary his mother, and they fell down and worshiped him. Then, opening their treasures, they offered him gifts, gold and frankincense and myrrh" (Matthew 2:9—11).

This story has to be seen as part of the ceremonial congratulations which follow a birth; in this case a king is congratulated by his subjects and therefore the greeting amounts to the paying of homage, and the presentation of gifts is part of the tradition. Such congratulations are typical of the Middle East even today. They are most certainly not meaningless gestures, but express a strong community feeling. The visit excellently expresses the relationship between the child and the wise men. It is considered an enormous insult to refrain from paying such a visit. Those who come to

Bethlehem are the simple shepherds, who are
of no social importance, and strangers. The
official representatives of the Jewish people—
the king, his advisers, and the notables of
Jerusalem—stay away. The evangelist Matthew makes use of the fact to indicate that
people are already divided about Jesus at the
time of his birth: the poor and rejected and the
Gentiles accept him, but he is repudiated by
his own people.

There has been much speculation about who
the Wise Men were. The Palestinian Justin
from Nablus (about A.D. 150) already assures
us that they came from "Arabia," which at
that time meant Transjordan, where the
Nabataeans dwelled. According to archaeological finds in this region, they paid a great deal
of attention to astrology. For instance, reliefs
have been found, representing the figures of
various gods who wear about their heads the
twelve signs of the zodiac as if they were
diadems. There were in the realm of the Nabataeans small Jewish communities living in
exile; and so predictions of the coming of the
Messiah cannot have been unknown among
the Gentiles. At this time Jerusalem did not by
any means exist as a ghetto, which the attitude
of a liberal king would have made impossible
anyway. On the Mount of Olives, Jewish os-
suaries containing the bones of the dead have
been found, on which the decorations were
definitely in the Transjordanian tradition
which must have been imported by alien craftsmen. The existence of wise men and their
presence in Jerusalem are historical fact. But
we know no details of what may have taken
place; that is a secret which God has not revealed. However, from the beginning, people
have been fascinated by the Wise Men, who
came unassumingly as simple pilgrims and not
in the manner of the splendid kings of the
Middle Ages.

Gregory of Tours (sixth century) reports
that in the floor of the apse of the Church of
the Nativity there is a large well from which
Mary is said to have drawn water. Into this
the star of the wise men is supposed to have
vanished. It is claimed that pious people can
still see it today, moving from side to side in
its orbit like the stars in the sky. This well,
which is really a cistern, was so well known to
the Crusaders that to them it was the feature

49

"And in that region there were shepherds out in the field, keeping watch over their flock by night" (Luke 2:8)

Bethlehem is adequately supplied with water. Its lush fields (below) provide pasture for flocks as in David's time. Shepherds pasturing their flocks were the first to know that Jesus was born in Bethlehem. A large fresco (right) in Shepherds' Field chapel shows the angel bringing the good tidings that the Messiah has been born.

Amongst the many archaeological finds in Shepherds' Field are remains of a Byzantine farm connected with a church and monastery which commemorated the angel's message.

distinguishing the town: "Bethlehem, where Christ was born, with the well into which the star descended after leading the wise men to their adoration of the child . . ."

In Luke the story of the birth is dominated by the figure of Augustus; in Matthew it is the figure of Herod which commands the account of the visit of the Wise Men. And this raises for us another question: Herod and Jesus—chance or design? It is difficult to imagine a greater contrast. Not far from Bethlehem lies the Herodium, already mentioned as the site of Herod's palace. It is a high plateau, half of which was raised by the labor of slaves. Excavations have revealed the remains of the palace, which was built partly into the hill. It possessed walls and towers, colonnaded court-yards, baths, and decorations in the style of Pompeii. Two hundred marble steps ascend to it. We must not allow the beauty of the Herodium to make us overlook the price in human suffering which must have been paid for its erection. Herod was cruel and unscrupulous and did not value human life; during his reign he ordered thousands to be executed. And only a few miles away Christ was born in

"A woman in the crowd... said to him, 'Blessed is the womb that bore you, and the breasts that you sucked!'"

(Luke 11:27)

Fearful of Herod who sought to take the life of the child Jesus, the Holy Family was forced to flee from Bethlehem to Egypt. This bas-relief of Mary nursing her infant can be seen in the Milk Grotto, Bethlehem.

a lowly cave; he came into the world for the sake of humanity, especially for all those who are poor, forsaken, and oppressed; he came to redeem them.

Herod was a very strange man: his fortress, incidentally like the fortress Machaerus east of the Dead Sea, lies on the fringe of civilization, on the edge of the mountainous desert. It is of no importance whatever either for defense or for trade and seems to have been built for purely personal reasons. Herod had enjoyed a Hellenstic-Roman upbringing and thought himself a man of the world; but with the Jews he also made pretence of being religiously minded. He liked occasionally to withdraw into the desert and he also wanted to be buried there. He came from Idumea, the southern part of Judea—from the town of Maresa—and perhaps these desires derive from his Eastern origins, conflicting with his otherwise modern attitudes. He was an unhappy man who suffered much inner conflict and was never at peace with himself. This explains why he was so very suspicious toward his own family and toward his subjects; he used to disguise himself at night in order to

According to legend, Mary suckled
her child in this cave
the Milk Grotto (left), before leaving
for Egypt. The Holy Family (right)
traveling into the desert.

spy on them. When he felt himself threatened by anyone he had him executed.

In an Apocryphal book which originated in the days of Jesus it says: "There followed a bold king, not descendant from a priestly family, who was presumptuous and wicked. He killed old and young, and the whole country was terribly afraid of him. He ravaged the people with slaughter, as had happened in Egypt" (Assumption of Moses 6:22). This text illustrates the murder of the infants in Bethlehem which the king ordered because he felt himself threatened by the newly born king of the Jews: "Then Herod . . . was in a furious rage, and he sent and killed all the male children in Bethlehem and in all that region who were two years old or under" (Matthew 2:16).

Afterward the evangelist cites the prophet Jeremiah: "A voice was heard in Ramah, wailing and loud lamentation, Rachel weeping for her children; she refused to be consoled, because they were no more" (Matthew 2:18). He refers to the tomb of Rachel, dating from before those times, on the way to Hebron, where the ancestress was venerated as the guardian of all mothers. The historical im-

plications of these words could not have been made plainer.

But the Holy Family had received a warning beforehand; in a dream Joseph heard the voice of God from the mouth of an angel: "'Rise, take the child and his mother, and flee to Egypt, and remain there till I tell you; for Herod is about to search for the child, to destroy him'" (Matthew 2:13).

Egypt, which was governed directly from Rome, had long been recognized as a place of refuge. There were numerous Jewish communities there, some of them quite large. The Gospel does not mention the name of the place where the family took refuge. According to an ancient tradition it is said to have been Heliopolis, north of Cairo. In the Church of St. Sergius in the old part of Cairo there is a crypt dating from the sixth century which is venerated as the dwelling place. In fact, Christianity very soon spread to Egypt; a papyrus has been discovered there with some verses from the Gospel According to St. John, which was almost certainly used in the liturgy and dates from the second century. There has always been close connection between the

55

country of the Nile and Palestine; it was confirmed by this flight. The journey must of course have been extremely difficult, as it led through the Negev and the Sinai Desert. Characteristic of the landscape there are the paths used by caravans and the Bedouin; to stray from them means most certainly to get lost. The Bible often talks of the good and the bad ways of life, and the Psalmist prays to God that he may keep him to the way of the righteous. This attitude refers back to the journey through the desert, when the people were conscious of God's presence and received their religion. Once Moses led the Children of Israel from slavery to the Promised Land. For the evangelist Matthew the return from Egypt is also a liberation, not from being enslaved by a certain country but from being enslaved by the world, in order to be led into the kingdom of God. Not for nothing does he quote the prophet Hosea: "Out of Egypt have I called my son" (Matthew 2:15).

Herod, who probably suffered from cancer, died a painful death in 4 B.C. and was buried in the Herodium. Joseph returned to the Land of Israel as God bade him: "But when he heard that Archelaus reigned over Judea in place of his father Herod, he was afraid to go there, and being warned in a dream he withdrew to the district of Galilee. And he went and dwelt in a city called Nazareth" (Matthew 2:22—23).

These few words reflect the history of the world at that time. Augustus divided Herod's kingdom among the three surviving sons: Archelaus, who had inherited his father's character and like him led a reign of terror, received Judea, Samaria, and Jerusalem; Antipas, always called by his family name Herod by the evangelists and whom we must therefore take care not to confuse with his father, became the ruler of Galilee and so actually the sovereign of Jesus; and Philippus reigned in the north in the region that is today called the Golan Heights. It contains the town named after him, Caesarea Philippi, today called Baniyas. Joseph probably came up the so-called royal highway along the Mediterranean coast leading via Gaza to the border of Judah; he may have continued north along the coast to avoid being apprehended by Archelaus. By Caesarea he would have turned east to cross the plain of Esdraelon in order to reach Nazareth. He would have seen, on this last stage of his journey, the green Carmel range full of ravines, the beauty of which is more than once celebrated in the Old Testament and which was sanctified especially through Elijah.

According to a tradition which has been proved to be no older than the Crusades, Mary is said to have taken refuge in a cave near Atlit; there is a similar tradition which originated at a much later date referring to the so-called Cave of the Prophets at the foot of Mount Carmel. What is certain is that the Holy Family did not cross the Carmel range, because this was territory in which pagan customs were practiced. But from the point of view of religion, this legendary suggestion is very significant, because it places geographically and in time the close connection which the New Testament sees between Jesus and Elijah, the precursor of the Messiah according to Jewish belief. It emphasizes the unity of the Old and the New Testament for all to see. In the same cave, the Moslems have worshiped Elijah since ancient times; the place reflects the ecumenical spirit which inspired Jesus, whose concern was the whole of mankind.

THE QUIET YEARS

Jesus lived in Nazareth for thirty years. While the Apocryphal books try to describe this time imaginatively, the Gospels are almost silent about it. These years were in a way a prelude to the time when he would appear in public with words and deeds, culminating in his death and his resurrection. With the greatest of awe we may perhaps dare to penetrate this silence, in order to gain a better understanding of all that happened subsequently. Luke reports: "And the child grew and became strong, filled with wisdom; and the favor of God was upon him" (2:40).

We can imagine the natural development of the child Jesus, which must have been similar to that of many other children. In the Middle East the child has a firm place within the family. We are continually told of three holy persons, even on official religious occasions, and so Joseph, Mary, and the child represent an indivisible unit. But they are part of a much larger family group, which also includes the "brothers and sisters" mentioned in the

"...(Joseph) took the child and his mother... and departed

Gospels, who according to Oriental custom, may be cousins more or less closely related. The most important relatives are Mary's cousin Elizabeth and her husband, the priest Zechariah, who are the parents of John the Baptist. Immediately after the annunciation by the angel, Mary visited Elizabeth, who showed a marvelous understanding of the blessing which had befallen Mary: "'Blessed are you among women, and blessed is the fruit of your womb! And why is this granted me, that the mother of my Lord should come to me?'" (Luke 1:42–43).

Mary answered with the famous song of praise, the Magnificat: "'My soul magnifies the Lord!'" (Luke 1:46).

The meeting of the two women represents a picture of ardor and faith which at the same time shows the closeness of their relationship.

According to Luke, this scene took place in an old town of Judah, which since ancient times has been identified as Ein Karem, about five miles away from Jerusalem. The present village is situated picturesquely within folds of hills and recalls an Italian place with its churches and monasteries, half obscured by pine groves. The Church of St. John the Baptist with the Grotto of the Nativity dates from the Byzantine period and is surrounded by a Roman-Herodian settlement. On the slopes of the western hill, not far from the spring, is the Church of the Visitation; in its crypt is a draw well, indicating that this building also dates from the Byzantine period.

That the family must have been very extensive can be deduced from the fact that in the third century, descendants of it were still living in Nazareth. At a trial in Asia Minor, the martyr Konon confessed to the Emperor Decius: "I come from the town of Nazareth in Galilee; I am related to Christ and in serving him I am following the tradition of my family." In the grotto of the Church of the Annunciation there is a mosaic dating from the fifth century with the inscription: FROM THE DEACON KONON IN JERUSALEM, who may have wished to honor his namesake in this way.

Joseph was a carpenter, and even if the Gospels do not state so explicity, it is highly likely that Jesus served him as an apprentice; according to the Talmud, a father is obliged

58

not only to support his son but also to teach him a trade. The division between ecclesiastic and secular occupations as we know it today did not exist at that time. On the contrary, boys studying the Talmud were expected also to practice a trade. Paul, for instance, was a tentmaker. As craftsmen frequently traveled about in search of work, a carpenter's apprentice would go where houses were being built, and so Jesus would have had the opportunity to get to know the surroundings of Nazareth and the inhabitants, with their troubles, their wants, their weaknesses, and their faults. Where Joseph dwelled with his family is not known. The caves, cisterns, silos, and winepresses over which the present Church of St. Joseph has been built present a graphic impression of the conditions in which people must then have lived — even if they cannot be identified as Joseph's house or his workshop.

Of much greater importance is the religious environment in which Jesus grew up. There must have been a group of devout Jews in Nazareth; if so, the family would have belonged to it. During the excavations of Caesarea a fragment of marble was found which bore a list of 24 families of priests, who served in turn in the temple at Jerusalem. It is the only inscription in which the name of Nazareth appears. One of the families must have made its home there — after having been driven from the capital by the Romans — doubtlessly because others who shared their faith lived there. Jesus received his first instruction at home. His father must have taught him the well-known *"Sh'ma"* (Hear, O Israel) as set down in Deuteronomy: "Hear, O Israel: The Lord our God is one Lord; and you shall love the Lord your God with all your heart, and with all your soul, and with all your might. And these words which I command you this day shall be upon your heart; and you shall teach them diligently to your children, and shall talk of them when you sit in your house, and when you walk by the way, and when you lie down, and when you rise. And you shall bind them as a sign upon your hand, and they shall be as frontlets between your eyes" (6:4–8).

Perhaps Jesus asked: "'What is the meaning of the testimonies and the statutes and the ordinances which the Lord our God has commanded you?'" And his father would have answered him: "'We were Pharaoh's slaves in Egypt; and the Lord brought us out of Egypt with a mighty hand; and the Lord showed signs and wonders, great and grievous, against Egypt and against Pharaoh and all his household, before our eyes; and he brought us out from there, that he might bring us in and give us the land which he swore to give to our fathers. And the Lord commanded us to do all these statutes, to fear the Lord our God, for our good always, that he might preserve us alive, as at this day. And it will be righteousness for us, if we are careful to do all this commandment before the Lord our God, as he has commanded us'" (Deuteronomy 6:20–25).

Every individual life was governed by prayer: "The Holy One, let us praise him." Of special importance were the prayers used at home; every meal began with a blessing said by the father over bread and wine and ended with a prayer of thanks and praise. The climax of the year was the Passover celebration, which ought actually to have been held in Jerusalem, where the heads of families slaughtered their lambs in the forecourt of the temple and then brought the meat home to be cooked and eaten. Outside Jerusalem, the celebration was shorter and did not include the killing of lambs. It was a festival especially for children, to whom the rites give the task of asking questions about its meaning. It also expressed the expectation of Messianic redemption, when the wine cups were filled for the third time during the meal — which was later to be of such significance during the Lord's Supper — and all those assembled prayed that the prophet Elijah might come and bring joyful tidings, help, and comfort to them, and that the merciful God might grant them the coming of the Messiah.

Christian households assemble to read the Bible; a Jewish family says many prayers together at home; this strengthens the Jewish religion and places the children firmly within the community. Then there are also the divine services held in the synagogue, where the ritual is confined to words; the cantor pronounces the *"Sh'ma,"* which is followed by the reading and an exposition of a passage

Sinai oases are characteristically marked by date groves. Traveling to Egypt, Jesus and his parents must have partaken of such sweet dates.

from the Torah and the prophets, and concluded with a blessing spoken by the priests. The synagogue is not only a holy place but also a place of assembly, in which the faithful meet and converse with one another. Each one is oriented toward Jerusalem to symbolize that all the ways lead to the Holy City. The shrine containing the Torah scrolls is accorded a special place, and so is the lectern; Jesus must early in life have become familiar with the holy texts and their Hebrew idiom. There were at that time many synagogues in Galilee; the earliest among those that have been preserved date from the third or fourth century. The first pilgrims mention a synagogue in Nazareth which later became a church. Where this building stood is uncertain. Perhaps the remains of a synagogue that have been found under the Church of the Annunciation are part of it.

The mature religious attitudes of Jesus, therefore, were influenced by the religious experiences of his childhood and by the education which he received in his youth. His habit of intimate prayer must have been encouraged by the tradition of family prayers.

When a scribe asked him which was the most important commandment, he answered unhesitatingly the *"Sh'ma."* In the synagogue he read from the prophet Isaiah (61:1 ff.) and expounded the text.

One event which occurred during these years deserves special emphasis. Yearly his parents made their pilgrimage to Jerusalem, and when Jesus was twelve years old they took him with them. Archelaus, the ruler of Judea, had been deposed and succeeded by Coponius; this was the first time that a Roman procurator had been appointed. Hence the journey had ceased to be dangerous. But the main reason why his parents took Jesus was that on his thirteenth birthday a young Jew becomes a Bar Mitzvah (literally: son of commandment) and from then on counts, as far as his religion is concerned, as an adult. He is allowed to read from the Torah in the synagogue and to ask questions about it. Therefore he had to make a true pilgrimage to the temple in Jerusalem.

What distinguishes a pilgrimage from any other journey is that it can be undertaken only by someone who lives in a foreign place, in

63

exile, and longs for his spiritual home. The Jews believed that God's presence was confined to the temple and their greatest desire was to be near him there. The pilgrim needs the company of other people who share his faith, with whom he can pray and sing together to prepare himself for the great adventure. A pilgrimage cannot be made alone; it is made by the family, the kinsfolk, the village, so that their community might be blessed.

The journey from Nazareth led through the hilly terrain of Samaria past the ancient capital of this region, called by Jeremiah "Samaria's green garland." It had been restored to magnificence by Herod, who named it Sebastos in honor of the Emperor Augustus. And then the road passed through Samaritan territory where the ancient town of Sichem lay in a valley between Mount Ebal and Mount Gerizim. Here the Samaritans sometimes expressed their hostility by refusing their hospitality to Jewish visitors. They were partly of mixed race; after the Assyrian conquest in 722 B.C. people from abroad settled among the Jewish population, so that the

Samaritans were not allowed to take part in the rebuilding of the temple when the Jews returned from exile. The Samaritans therefore built their own temple on Mount Gerizim and brought sacrifices there according to the local tradition. Samaritanism was primarily a sect within Judaism with affinities with the Sadducees as well as with the Qumran community. The Old Testament shows us the variety, diversity and something of the tensions within Judaism between North and South, Samaria and Jerusalem. The beginnings of Samaritanism as a separate body characteristic of an isolated mountain region can be brought down to the third or second century B.C. Today, about 300 Samaritans still live in this district, annually celebrating the Passover on their hill according to their own interpretation of the Torah. And here Jesus was confronted not only with the problem of where God ought to be worshiped — in Jerusalem or on Mount Gerizim — but also with the fact that this dispute caused tension among people, leading the Jews to despise the Samaritans. The story of the good Samaritan and the conversation with the

The Church of St. Joseph was built in 1914. It stands on the site where the Holy Family lived, some 2,000 years ago.

woman of Samaria (John 4:7–26) show that the problem disturbed Jesus, who saw its solution in the sincere love for one's fellowmen and in his own mission as the savior of the world.

This was also the place of Jacob's well, where the caravans have paused since ancient times, keeping alive the memory of Jacob, who dug the well in a field. Near it the bones of Joseph which the children of Israel had brought with them from Egypt lay buried. Almost certainly, the pilgrims rested here. There were such resting places, a day's journey apart, along the whole route. The last of them, about ten miles outside Jerusalem, today is the village of El-Bireh, which has a spring and a mosque. Soon afterward they had a magnificent view of the town, with its protective walls and its radiant temple visible for miles, and the psalm which they must have sung so often suddenly became reality:

I was glad when they said to me,
　　"Let us go to the house of the Lord!"
Our feet have been standing
　　within your gates, O Jerusalem!

66

"...*they returned... to their own city, Nazareth. And the*

child grew and became strong, filled with wisdom'' (Luke 2:39–40)

There were many house-caves in the mountainous areas of the Holy Land. Tradition has it that in one (left), beneath the Church of St. Joseph, Jesus was reared. Three frescos decorate the apses of St. Joseph's Church. One (right) depicts the Holy Family.

Jerusalem, built as a city
    which is bound firmly together,
to which the tribes go up,
    the tribes of the Lord,
as was decreed for Israel,
    to give thanks to the name of the Lord.
There thrones for judgment were set,
    the thrones of the house of David.

Pray for the peace of Jerusalem!
    "May they prosper who love you!
Peace be within your walls
    and security within your towers!"
For my brethren and companions' sake
    I will say, "Peace be within you!"
For the sake of the house of the Lord our God,
    I will seek your good.

                (Psalm 122).

It is characteristic of the Middle East that certain places have remained holy throughout the centuries, although another religion may have taken possession of them. Today the Moslem Dome of the Rock in Jerusalem is a center of attraction, as the Jewish temple once was. When Jesus came to Jerusalem, the

"And when he was twelve years old, they went up (to Jerusalem) according to custom" *(Luke 2:42)*

This is how the Jerusalem temple looked in Jesus' time, according to a reconstruction recently made in Jerusalem. Within, at the age of twelve, he gave proof of his knowledge of the Law to Jerusalem teachers.

temple had just been magnificently rebuilt by Herod. The temple area had been very much enlarged to a size of some thirty-five acres. Around it were double colonnades. The Jewish historian Josephus describes them thus: "All the cloisters were double, and the pillars to them belonging were twenty-five cubits in height, and supported the cloisters. These pillars were of one entire stone each of them, and that stone was white marble; and the roofs were adorned with cedar, curiously graven. The natural magnificence, and excellent polish, and the harmony of the joints in these cloisters, afforded a prospect that was very remarkable; nor was it on the outside adorned with any work of the painter or engraver. The cloisters (of the outmost court) were in breadth thirty cubits, while the entire compass of it was by measure six furlongs, including the tower of Antonia; those entire courts that were exposed to the air were laid with stones of all sorts" (*Jewish War* 5, 5, 2).

The eastern portico was named after Solomon; that to the south, dominating the Valley of Kidron, was called "Royal." On the east side the area was bounded by the so-

called pinnacle of the temple, mentioned in the story of the temptation of Jesus (Matthew 4:5). There were eight gates leading into the temple, including the two Huldah, or "mole," gates from the south, which passed underneath the Royal Porch. To the east was the Gate of Susa, still visible as the Golden Gate which was walled up by the Byzantines. In the western wall was the main gate named the Gate of Coponius after the first procurator; it was decorated with the golden eagle as a sign that the temple had been placed under the protection of Rome. Anyone was allowed to enter the outer area, which was therefore the Court of the Gentiles. The actual temple was enclosed by a balustrade, and at the entrances to it were warning notices, one of which is now in a museum in Istanbul. It says that foreigners have freedom of access provided they do not go beyond the balustrade which went all around the central edifice and which no uncircumcised could cross without incurring the death penalty. Fourteen steps led through the Beautiful Gate to the Court of the Women where the poor boxes were, into one of which the poor widow cast her two mites (Luke 21:1–4). Another fifteen steps led up to the famous Gate of Nicanor, to which Mary had brought the child at the time of his presentation; this led through the Court of the Men to that of the priests, which had in its center the altar for the burnt offerings and to the left of it a large basin called the Brazen Sea resting upon twelve bulls cast in bronze.

Further steps led up to the actual temple, a comparatively small building. A priceless curtain, emboidered with a map of the known world, concealed from view what lay beyond, and none except the priest on duty was allowed to go farther. It contained the golden altar at which incense was offered and next to it the seven-branched candelabrum and the table with the twelve loaves of shewbread, which were replaced by fresh ones every sabbath. Beyond it, behind another large curtain, lay the Holy of Holies, which none except the high priest was allowed to enter, and he only on the Day of Atonement. A stone designated the place where once the Ark of the Covenant had stood.

It may be imagined that Jesus received an awesome impression of the temple — the sole place of God's presence. In Solomon's Porch the boy argued with the rabbis, astonishing them with his questions and with his answers. He remained behind when his parents left, and when his worried mother at last found him he said to her enigmatically: "'Did you not know that I must be in my Father's house?'" (Luke 2:49).

It is one of the most original sayings of Jesus, in which he speaks of God for the first time as his father and so reveals the secret of his descent. Today the western wall, the so-called Wailing Wall, is all that remains of the ancient walls of Herod's temple; one can still see the pilaster and the beginning of the so-called Robinson's Arch, which was part of a large viaduct leading to the upper town. Excavations in 1967, led by the well-known archaeologist Benjamin Mazar, revealed the cornerstone. Adjacent to it on the southern side remain traces of the road from which the pilgrims entered the gates.

RETURN TO NAZARETH

The next years spent in Nazareth passed unmarked by external events. The people around

Jesus did not know who he was: but Mary stored all that happened in her heart. It was for him a time of observing the world, watching the sower at his work, walking through fields in which the grain stood high. Perhaps he climbed a watchtower in the vineyards at the time of the grape harvest or lingered where the shepherds tended their flocks. He was familiar with the secrets of the fig tree, the briar, the sycamore, and the mustard seed which develops into a large bush, as well as with the ways of the foxes and the places of the birds' nests. All this was for him a manifestation of the glory of God, which he made use of later when he filled his parables with images drawn from nature.

Above all, he observed people, who for him were the children of God; he endeavored to talk with people. The poor and rejected, the suffering and the mourners, as well as strangers such as the Samaritans, interested him particularly. On the eastern shore of the Sea of Galilee he met Greeks in the towns of Hippos (near Ein Gev) Gadara (near Umm Qeis) and Gergesa. Palestinians, living in a country that is a gateway, have always been familiar with foreign languages. Today every Arab boy has a smattering of English and Hebrew. People here have a good ear and a retentive memory, which makes it easy for them to acquire and retain foreign phrases. In everyday life Jesus spoke Aramaic; his prayers he said in Hebrew. Since he was able to talk to Pilate without an interpreter, we may assume that he also knew a certain amount of Greek.

We know little about his actual appearance. No contemporary picture exists; in Byzantine mosaics he is represented according to theological conceptions. His garments were those usual at that time: a sleeveless gown covered by another, sandals, and a staff. His head may have been covered by a white cloth, similar to an Arab *kaffiyeh* held in place with a cord, as a protection against the heat and the dust. Typical of the inhabitants of this land are large dark eyes, which are often profound and look compassionately at their fellowmen but sometimes express fear when something unexpected occurs. These characteristic eyes make one realize why the act of looking plays such an important part in the Bible. But the local people are also reserved and do not betray their feelings. One never hears loud laughter. It is never said of Jesus that he laughed; looking at the young man searching for eternal life, he expresses his affection for him with a smile. Occasionally people weep in a quiet, reserved way, and especially men weep like that when they have suffered a great personal loss, when someone has died. Jesus wept for Jerusalem and also when Lazarus died. But the people soon regain their self-control and only the sadness of their eyes reflects that they have cause to mourn. The voice of Jesus must have been extraordinary; people "wondered at the gracious words which proceeded out of his mouth" (Luke 4:22). His voice was effective, and so was his manner of speaking — for instance, when he called Lazarus from his grave (John 11:43).

How much Jesus knew of what was going on in the world we can only deduce from certain indications. They would have heard in Nazareth of the death of the former governor of Syria, Quinctilius Varus, who sent the rebels of nearby Sepphoris into slavery and had 2,000 resistance fighters crucified. The Emper-

Just before flowing into the Dead Sea, the Jordan River makes the surrounding desert bloom. Here, John baptized Jesus.

74

f Galilee and was baptized by John in the Jordan'' (Mark 1:9)

or Augustus died when Jesus was twenty years old; it was the image of his successor Tiberius which was on the Roman denarius which the Pharisees showed to Jesus when they asked him whether it was right to pay the taxes. Tiberius' second in command was the anti-Semite Seian, chief of the imperial guard, who made things difficult for the local population. New procurators were brought to Judea. Among them, taking fifth place, was Pontius Pilate (A D 26–36/37). He lived in Caesarea Maritima, and his name has been found inscribed on a stone among the ruins of the Roman amphitheater. Already before his time there had arisen a pontifical crisis in Jerusalem because the procurators had begun to appoint and dismiss the high priests according to whim. Caiaphas, who was to lead the proceedings against Jesus, was appointed to his post when Jesus was twenty-five years old. That the evangelists were thoroughly familiar with contemporary events is apparent from Luke: "In the fifteenth year of the reign of Tiberius Caesar, Pontius Pilate being governor of Judea, and Herod being tetrarch of Galilee, and his brother Philip tetrarch of the region of Ituraea and Trachonitis, and Lysanias tetrarch of Abilene, in the high-priesthood of Annas and Caiaphas..." (3:1–2).

THE SHORES OF THE RIVER JORDAN

At the beginning of the year 28 Jesus appeared by the Jordan; he had left the quiet life of Nazareth behind him. A multitude had been attracted by John the Baptist: "John the baptizer appeared in the wilderness, preaching a baptism of repentance for the forgiveness of sins. And there went out to him all the country of Judea, and all the people of Jerusalem; and they were baptized by him in the river Jordan, confessing their sins. Now John was clothed with camel's hair, and had a leather girdle around his waist, and ate locusts and wild honey" (Mark 1:4–6).

He belonged to the ancient line of prophets, proclaiming the imminence of the judgment by means of images that were familiar to all from their daily lives: "But when he saw many of the Pharisees and Sadducees coming for baptism, he said to them, 'You brood of vipers! Who warned you to flee from the wrath to come? Bear fruit that befits repent-

"...he fasted forty days and forty nights, and afterward he was hungry" *(Matthew 4:2)*

Jesus fasted for forty days before beginning his public preaching. In the end, the devil sought to deflect him from his holy purpose. Legend has it that Jesus sat on this stool-shaped rock, resisting Satan's temptations. It is now kept in a monastery on the Hill of the Temptation, near Jericho.

ance, and do not presume to say to yourselves, "We have Abraham as our father"; for I tell you, God is able from these stones to raise up children to Abraham. Even now the axe is laid to the root of the trees; every tree therefore that does not bear good fruit is cut down and thrown into the fire'" (Matthew 3:7–10).

That God in his mercy allowed his people certain privileges — for instance, the descent from Abraham — is no reason for complacency; on the contrary, it is necessary for each individual to repent and to acknowledge the living God. When the unknown Jesus approached, the seer exclaimed: "After me comes he who is mightier than I, the thong of whose sandals I am not worthy to stoop down and untie. I have baptized you with water; but he will baptize you with the Holy Spirit" (Mark 1:7–8).

John's baptism cleansed people and symbolized their conversion, but baptism by the Messiah would invest them with the spirit signifying a new life. And now approached the memorable moment in which Jesus was baptized by John: "In those days Jesus came from Nazareth of Galilee and was baptized

"...Jesus was led up by the Spirit into the wilderness to be tempted by the devil"

(Matthew 4:1)

In early times, hermits built a cliff-hanging monastery on the Hill of the Temptation, marking Jesus' fast in this place. It is now known as the "Mount of Quarantine" (Forty).

by John in the Jordan. And when he came up out of the water, immediately he saw the heavens opened and the Spirit descending upon him like a dove; and a voice came from heaven, 'Thou art my beloved Son; with thee I am well pleased'" (Mark 1:9–11).

The Jordan is a very special river. It twists and turns as it winds its way through the deepest valley on earth. In spite of its ample waters, the river had no economic significance in antiquity; but neither was it a great natural barrier, hardly interfering with passing traffic. Especially in summertime it can be forded quite easily. But from a religious point of view it holds a unique position. In his book *The River Jordan*, Nelson Glueck, a well-known archaeologist, expresses it like this: "Its basic importance cannot be magnified, because its role in history has been great beyond all rational measurement; it is in connection with the revelation of the divine that the importance of the Jordan becomes paramount, exceeding that of any other river in the world." Its waters are not renowned for their healing powers, as are those of some other rivers. It obtains its significance from

78

The remains of an ancient synagogue in Nazareth, said to have been Jesus' school and the scene of his first preaching in Galilee. Once, when he applied a passage from the book of Isaiah to himself, the audience grew so angered that his very life was endangered.

the fact that it is the boundary of the Promised Land. For Jacob, crossing the Jordan is a decisive event, because he is returning to the land promised to the patriarchs; Moses is not allowed to go beyond it; only Joshua is allowed to lead the people in a solemn procession into the country which God had promised their ancestors he would grant them. In Deuteronomy, therefore, the act of crossing the river is considered to be of great significance: "Hear, O Israel; you are to pass over the Jordan this day... Know therefore this day that he who goes over before you... is the Lord your God" (9:1, 3).

And so the entry into the Land of Canaan is indeed a "transition," not only in the literal but also in the religious sense; it proves that the people have been under God's guidance all along, and that they have now come into his possession. In a similar way, the baptism in the Jordan is a turning point; the Holy Ghost has descended upon Jesus and the voice of his Heavenly Father has acknowledged him as God's Son; now he is ready to begin his task of leading the people into the kingdom of God. The baptism probably took place on the east bank of the river. According to John 1:28, John the Babtist was active in Bethany beyond the Jordan, and he may very well have chosen the ford which according to Joshua 3:14–16 the Children of Israel used as a crossing. After the conquest by the Arabs, Christian imagination transferred the baptism to the west bank, which is lined with the chapels and convents of the various rites. From earliest times, pilgrims have come here to take away a little water for the baptism of their relatives and friends. On the occasion of the Festival of the Epiphany of the Lord, Greek Orthodox Christians come in thousands to the river to renew their baptism in the water symbolically, and Catholics sing from a boat passages from the Gospels telling of the baptism of Christ.

After the baptism Jesus withdrew into the desert to fast and pray according to the example that John the Baptist had set him; this was the occasion on which the devil tempted him (Luke 4:1–13). According to a pious tradition which originated at a later date, he sat on a mountain, meditating and regarding the valley before him; but in fact

"And they... led him to the brow of the hill on which their city was built, that they might throw him down headlong" (Luke 4:29)

The Mount of the Precipitation. Legend has it that it was from this crag that Jesus' fellow-citizens sought to cast him down. Nowadays, the incident is sited above Nazareth's own valley, within the town limits.

he must have wandered about in the desert, crossing barren ridges and deep wadis. The desert is a place of grace, because it reveals the magnitude and majesty of creation, which is reflected in the landscape and in man; but in its desolation and loneliness it is also a place of temptation. Naturally, soon afterward the attempt was made to place the event geographically. According to the Apocryphal Gospel of the Hebrews, it happened on Mount Tabor, possibly chosen for theological reasons to symbolize the victory of Jesus over Satan by the landscape. Since the Byzantine period, the sheer cliff to the west of the oldest part of Jericho has been acknowledged as the site of the temptation. Numerous grottoes, both natural and man-made, soon began to attract hermits and monks; among the most distinguished of them were St. Chariton and St. Elpidius, who wished to live in Biblical places after the manner of the Lord. Halfway up the hillside, a Greek convent perches like an aerie. A cave there which has been turned into a chapel is said to have been one of the places where Jesus dwelled.

The story may give the impression that what John the Baptist was doing was extraordinary and even unique. This may well have been the effect that he created. But there were in fact many who preached repentance at that time. Many religious people longing for the coming of the Messiah dwelled in the Judean desert and the region of the Dead Sea. In 1947 a Bedouin boy accidentally discovered near the Wadi Qumran a pot in which ancient writings had been preserved. A thorough and systematic search of the region was then made, and eleven further caves yielded many valuable literary finds. A hill containing traces of a settlement was excavated, and it was revealed that a Jewish community had dwelled there in seclusion. Since then, Qumran has become a significant name, famous far beyond the narrow circle of Biblical scholars. The finds are of importance because they provide an independent testimony of Judaism at the time of Christ. Qumran represents one of the numerous sects of Judaism which existed side by side during that period, just as they still exist in Christianity today. That very little had been known about these groups made Qumran all the more important; perhaps its signific-

"And he (Jesus) went about all Galilee, teaching in their synagogues and preaching the gospel of the kingdom..."

(Matthew 4:23)

The wooded hills of Galilee were the scene of much of Jesus' public ministry.

ance has been a little exaggerated. In place and time John and Jesus must have been very close to Qumran, and this made it necessary to consider the possibility that they were influenced by it. There have been scholars who have attempted to trace the origin of Christianity to Qumran. But if we consider some of the texts from Qumran and from the Gospels side by side, great differences between them become apparent.

The sect at Qumran said in prayer: "The abundance of his mercies toward all the sons of his grace" (Hymn 4:33).

Only a few miles away the choir of the angels in the fields of Bethlehem sang: "Glory to God in the highest, and on earth peace among men of his grace."

Qumran looks back to the covenant which God made with his people; Bethlehem looks toward the present time, in which the Word dwells among us.

The teachings of Jesus center on the love for our fellowmen: "'But I say to you, Love your enemies and pray for those who persecute you'" (Matthew 5:44).

But in Qumran a teaching said: "That they may love all that he has chosen and hate all that he has rejected" (Community Rule 1:4).

In Qumran, a strict line was drawn between the chosen people and others: "And no man smitten with any human uncleanness shall enter the assembly of God; no man smitten in his flesh or paralyzed in his feet or hands or lame or blind or deaf or dumb or smitten in his flesh with a visible blemish; no old and tottery man unable to stand still in the midst of the congregation; none of these shall come to hold office among the congregation of the man" (Messianic Rule 2:5).

But Jesus gave these instructions: "'Go out quickly to the streets and lanes of the city, and bring in the poor and maimed and blind and lame'" (Luke 14:21).

In Qumran, much importance was attached to the order of precedence: "Each man shall sit in his place: the priests shall sit first and the elders second, and all the rest of the people according to their rank" (Community Rule 6:8). In the so-called Chapter Hall, the place reserved for the superior is specially marked with a circle of stones, still visible today.

84

But Jesus called to his people: "'So the last will be first, and the first last'" (Matthew 20:16).

One of the greatest interests of Jesus was missionary, and it was shared by John the Baptist in his own different way: "'Go therefore and make disciples of all nations, baptizing them in the name of the Father and of the Son and of the Holy Spirit'" (Matthew 28:19).

The sect of Qumran rejected all contact with the rest of the world. The newcomer who wished to become a member of the community was commanded not to enter into conversation with those who were corrupt and to withhold from them the teachings of the commandments.

There are also many important sayings of Jesus which do not have their counterpart in Qumran: "'And he who does not take his cross and follow me is not worthy of me'" (Matthew 10:38). "'I am the resurrection and the life; he who believes in me, though he die, yet shall he live, and whoever lives and believes in me shall never die'" (John 11:25–26).

Many similarities can be explained by the common Jewish origin; the differences were created by the person of Jesus, by his crucifixion and his resurrection. In Qumran, everything centered on the observance and the interpretation of the Torah; with Jesus, the focal point is his personality, before which all precepts and examples must surrender their absolute value. Jesus says: "'So it is lawful to do good on the sabbath'" (Matthew 12:12).

It is likely that Jesus knew the community at Qumran at least from hearsay; it is unlikely that he had anything to do with it, for its teachings do not at all agree with his own. John the Baptist is a little closer to Qumran in spirit. It is possible that in his youth he belonged to the community for a time but later cut himself off from it because he was concerned with preaching repentance and converting people, while the sect at Qumran had withdrawn from the world and shunned public activity.

Jesus and Qumran — chance or design? To ask this question is to emphasize the problem of the co-existence of Judaism and Christianity. But at the same time it demonstrates

86

"Consider the lilies, how they grow; they neither toil nor spin" *(Luke 12:27)*

Springtime in the Holy Land brings a feast for the eye and joy for the soul. All Galilee is in bloom and the Sea of Galilee forms a vision in blue. Jesus often illustrated his teaching by references to such wonders of nature.

that there were at that time Jewish people of profound faith who sought salvation in the solitude of the desert and whose way of life anticipated that of the Christian hermits and monks in the Judean desert.

THE MARRIAGE IN CANA

Soon after his baptism Jesus and his mother attended a farmer's wedding at Cana in Galilee. According to the prevailing custom, such festivities beginning the third day of the week (John 2:1) usually lasted seven days, and the hosts ran out of wine: "When the wine failed, the mother of Jesus said to him, 'They have no wine.' And Jesus said to her, 'O woman, what have you to do with me? My hour has not yet come.' His mother said to the servants, 'Do whatever he tells you.' Now six stone jars were standing there, for the Jewish rites of purification, each holding twenty or thirty gallons. Jesus said to them, 'Fill the jars with water.' And they filled them up to the brim. He said to them, 'Now draw some out, and take it to the steward of the feast.' So they took it. When the steward of the feast tasted the water now become wine,

88

and did not know where it came from... the steward of the feast called the bridegroom and said to him, 'Every man serves the good wine first; and when men have drunk freely, then the poor wine; but you have kept the good wine until now'" (John 2:3–10).

The evangelist explicitly adds: "This, the first of his signs, Jesus did at Cana in Galilee, and manifested his glory; and his disciples believed in him."

The effect of this first manifestation of Jesus' powers is that of a demonstration. He was not an ascetic, who might lead a retired life in the desert; he went among plain simple people to bring them joy. Certainly the emphasis ought not to be placed on the actual miracle, which helped poor people to overcome a temporary embarrassment, but on the profound, enigmatical meaning of the story, illuminating the person of Christ, who is the grapevine and the life, which he will surrender when the time is ripe. The steward's comment to the bridegroom, that he has kept the good wine in reserve, may sound to the superficial listener like a joke; but if we reflect upon it we realize its profound religious significance. Here in Cana, at the very beginning of his public ministry, Jesus revealed himself as very different from the community at Qumran, very different also from John the Baptist — Jesus is unique.

About seven miles from Nazareth, on the way to the Sea of Galilee, in the midst of pomegranate and olive groves lies the Arab village Cana, dominated by a Latin church with a red cupola and twin towers. In its crypt are replicas of a few earthenware pots. The place must date back to very early times, because the remains of an ancient synagogue have been found there. But there is also another place which claims to have been the site of the first miracle performed by Jesus: it is a hill not far from Cana, which shows traces of having once been inhabited; it has not yet been excavated. But these conflicting claims are of purely archaeological and topographical interest. Much more important is the typically Oriental picture presented by the modern Cana; the town which existed in the lifetime of Jesus must have looked a little like this.

90

THE FIRST PASSOVER IN JERUSALEM

Soon afterward, Jesus attended the celebration of Passover in Jerusalem and attracted public attention: "In the temple he found those who were selling oxen and sheep and pigeons, and the money-changers at their business. And making a whip of cords, he drove them all, with the sheep and oxen, out of the temple; and he poured out the coins of the money-changers and overturned their tables. And he told those who sold the pigeons, 'Take these things away; you shall not make my Father's house a house of trade'" (John 2:14–16).

As the taxes for the temple had to be paid on this occasion, the money-changers had come into the forecourts together with those who sold the animals for the sacrifice. Jesus was concerned with preserving the purity of the temple rites, and his behavior was justified. Nevertheless, the event caused a disturbance; the temple police appeared and questioned him: "'What sign have you to show us for doing this?'" (John 2:18).

Jesus answered them enigmatically: "'Destroy this temple, and in three days I will raise it up'" (John 2:19).

His listeners naturally thought he was referring to the temple built of stone standing before them, while Jesus was thinking of his body, which would rise again after his violent death. The first misunderstanding had occurred.

In this period the meeting took place between Jesus and Nicodemus, a Pharisee and a member of the Sanhedrin, the supreme council and tribunal of the Jews. The encounter grants us a glimpse of the diversity of the religious parties of that time. The expectation of the imminent coming of the Messiah was a characteristic which they all shared, but beliefs about it differed. The Zealots were idealists and at the same time intensely nationalistic; they believed that deliverance should be brought about by political revolt. Priests and the lay aristocracy belonged mostly to the sect of the Sadducees. They believed in the strict observance of the Torah and rejected the so-called Tradition of the Fathers. Their theological teachings were quite unambiguous; they rejected the resurrection of the dead, the immortality of the soul, and the doctrine of reward and punish-

Cana lies in a small valley north-east of Nazareth and has preserved its Oriental character. Jesus and Mary were guests at a wedding feast in the hamlet.

ment in a life beyond. They were well known for their strict administration of justice, which followed the rule "an eye for an eye and a tooth for a tooth."

In the time of Jesus they lost much of their influence to the Pharisees. The latter were the "separatists," rejecting all non-Jewish and especially all Hellenistic influences. They endeavored to keep themselves pure, and for this reason tax collectors, sinners, harlots, and others were unable to become members of their sect. Their aim was that "the true Israel" should become manifest in daily life. The supreme guiding principle was the law, but it had to be interpreted according to changing economic and political conditions. For this the scribes, who belonged to the petty bourgeois (tradespeople, craftsmen, day laborers) and whose influence derived from their knowledge of the law, were necessary. When the Wise Men of the East appeared at Herod's court and the king asked them where the new king of the Jews had been born, the scribes answered at once with a quotation from the prophet Micah. They were highly respected because they had spent many years studying, and they were the experts in the field of justice, its propagators and administrators. They bore the honorable title of rabbi. They endeavored to match the law to the individual events of everyday life, provided numerous rules of behavior worded as commandments and prohibitions, and in the course of this work developed an admirable casuistry. Since they believed that it was possible to observe the law, they rejected the judgment preached by the Baptist and the call of Jesus to repent.

The story of the Pharisee and the tax collector provides a good example of what the Pharisees stood for: "'Two men went up into the temple to pray, one a Pharisee and the other a tax collector. The Pharisee stood and prayed thus with himself, "God, I thank thee that I am not like other men, extortioners, unjust, adulterers, or even like this tax collector. I fast twice a week, I give tithes of all that I get." But the tax collector, standing far off, would not even lift his eyes to heaven, but beat his breast, saying, "God, be merciful to me a sinner!" I tell you, this man went down

to his house justified rather than the other'"
(Luke 18:10–14).

This Pharisee was certainly a devout and honest man who took his religion seriously. He had no ulterior motive for maintaining that he fasted twice weekly and paid his tithes; he was no hypocrite. He was convinced that he did everything necessary for his own salvation. His plain statement confirmed it. But he confronted the presence of God with a sort of monologue on the theme of himself; he referred to himself repeatedly. The tax collector, on the other hand, said very little; he did not state facts but addressed God directly: he was looking for a dialogue with God. The piety of the Pharisee was petrified, lifeless; the tax collector, though doubtlessly a sinner, possessed a vital faith — he wanted to enter into a close personal relationship with God.

A monologue and a dialogue — it indicates the huge differences which divide Jesus from the Pharisees. This explains why Jesus fought against the strict observance of the sabbath, the purification laws, fasts, and routine prayers. In the Gospels, the Pharisees are represented as hypocrites, and the contrast between their theories and practices is criticized. It has to be remembered that this applies to any religion once its living observance becomes a fixed formula. Not only Jewry but all religious communities are exposed to this threat. The problems which the Pharisees present to Jesus are revealed in the conversation between him and Nicodemus, who does not understand that he needs to be reborn "of water and of the Spirit" (John 3:5) in order to see the kingdom of God.

JESUS IN GALILEE

For some time after Passover, Jesus remained in the region where his baptism had taken place, but then he returned to Galilee. The reason for this was that the Pharisees had begun to suspect him, because he had collected more followers than John. Jesus wished to avoid an open conflict with his opponents and therefore thought it better to withdraw. Also, news got about of the arrest of the Baptist; he had publicly accused Herod Antipas of adultery and was imprisoned in the fortress of Machaerus east of the Dead Sea. The journey

"On the third day there was a marriage at Cana in Galilee, and the mother of Jesus was there; Jesus also was invited to the marriage with his disciples" (John 2:1–2)

The Latin Church, Cana (left), modeled after the cathedral in Salzburg, Austria, commemorates Jesus' first miracle when he turned water into wine. A pitcher (right) recalls the first miracle.

"Jesus said to them, 'Fill the jars with water'" (John 2:7)

97

"As he walked by the Sea of Galilee, he saw two brothers, Simon who is called Peter and Andrew his brother, casting a net into the sea..." (Matthew 4:18)

Most of Jesus' public life was spent in the neighborhood of the Sea of Galilee (left). It is also known as Lake Tiberias, Lake Kinnereth and Lake Gennesareth. Many residents of the area gain a livelihood from fishing (below) in this wellstocked lake. Jesus' audiences often included fishermen of the region.

led Jesus once more through Samaria and provided the occasion for his famous conversation with the woman of Samaria by Jacob's well. Having asked her for a drink of water, he revealed himself as the living water which shall become within human beings "a spring of water welling up to eternal life" (John 4:6–26). This well was already a sacred place in the time of Jesus, for Jacob and his children and his cattle had drunk from it, as the woman of Samaria said to Jesus. It goes down about thirty-five yards to reach fresh underground water. For Christians, this well early became associated with the Lord. In the time of St. Jerome there was already a church there. The Crusaders built a basilica with three naves; two flights of stairs led down to the crypt, which was all that remained after the church fell into ruin in the course of time. Before the First World War there were plans to erect a new building; only the outer walls of it exist.

BY THE SEA OF GALILEE

Now Jesus began his public ministry in Galilee. The evangelist Mark, basing his account on that of Peter, describes it thus: "The time is fulfilled, and the kingdom of God is at hand; repent, and believe in the gospel" (Mark 1:15).

As the kingdom of God was initiated by Jesus, the time which God had decided upon had been fulfilled. For humanity, this was the hour of decision, demanding a conversion of thought and intention, and faith in Jesus Christ. His ministry revolved around the fresh-water lake called the Sea of Galilee. In the New Testament, it is also called the Lake of Tiberias, Lake Kinnereth and by other names. The river Jordan passes through the lake, which lies 686 feet below sea level. The landscape around it is unique. To the east and to the west the ground rises steeply to a fertile plateau; from a height, the water appears a very deep blue. From the southern shore one can see the twin peaks of Mount Canaan with the town of Safed; at night its bright lights remind one of Jesus' reference to a city on a hill (Matthew 5:14). In the distance rises the snow-covered Mount Hermon, with its different colors apparently belonging to another world. On the eastern shore gleam the small white houses of kibbutz Ein Gev; beyond it

100

rises the hill which was the site of the Hellenistic town Hippos. The charming bay of Magdala lies on the northwestern shore, and between Tabgha and Capernaum, the groves of willow and eucalyptus trees appear like oases. But the impression of romantic solitude and barrenness is misleading. In ancient times the whole district was one vast orchard, which is slowly being restored by the new settlements.

Josephus describes it thus: "The country that lies over against the lake had the same name of Gennesareth; its nature is wonderful as well as its beauty; its soil is so fruitful that all sorts of trees can grow upon it, and the inhabitants accordingly plant all sorts of trees there; for the temper of the air is so well mixed, that it agrees very well with those several sorts, particularly walnuts, which require the coldest air; there are palm trees also which grow best in hot air; fig trees also and olives grow near them, which yet require an air that is more temperate. One may call this place the ambition of nature, where it forces those plants that are naturally enemies to one another to agree together; it is a happy contention of the seasons, as if every one of them laid claim to this country, for it not only nourishes different sorts of autumnal fruit beyond men's expectation, but preserves them a great while. It supplies men with the principal fruits, with grapes and figs continually during ten months of the year and the rest of the fruit as they become ripe together through the whole year; for besides the good temperature of the air, it is also watered from a most fertile fountain" (*Jewish War*, 3, 10, 8).

It has been said in the Talmud that the fruit there ripens as fast as deer can run and that one could eat a hundred pieces of it and still wish for more; because this fruit is so very sweet it has to be followed by something spicy, eaten perhaps with bread.

The boulders of black basalt covering the whole hillside are typical of a landscape which was once volcanic; they are sometimes used as building material and make the houses appear dark and sinister. The black Roman theater by the ruins of Gadara, situated above the level of the lake to the south of it, and even more the synagogue of Chorazin above Capernaum, provide a dark backcloth in

Jesus often preached in the synagogue of Capernaum, his second home. In the town he performed cures for the benefit of many, amongst others, the mother-in-law of Peter and the servant of the Roman centurion.

glistening sunlight to the words of the Lord: "'Woe to you, Chorazin! Woe to you, Bethsaida! for if the mighty works done in you had been done in Tyre and Sidon, they would have repented long ago in sackcloth and ashes'" (Matthew 11:21).

The lake itself — the water is pure enough to drink — is generally calm. But sometimes sudden and dangerous storms turn it into a raging sea with high waves. The lake yields an extraordinary amount of fish. Perhaps the best known is St. Peter's fish; its male carry the eggs and the young in their mouths. It was given its name because the coin Peter found was carried in the mouth of such a fish. The lake is alive with many fishing vessels and looks especially beautiful at night when they set out with their lamps alight; during the day the fishermen may be seen repairing their nets on the shore. We can easily imagine that Jesus often went by boat from one side of the lake to the other.

In the time of Jesus there were a great many towns and villages by the lake, especially on the western shore. Tiberias, which is today the most important town, is mentioned in the

Gospels only in passing. It was founded near hot springs by Herod Antipas in honor of the Roman emperor; a bathing hut dating back to antiquity can still be seen there today. But as part of the town was built over an ancient cemetery, it was avoided by orthodox Jews as unclean and only achieved some importance after Jerusalem had been destroyed. This explains why it plays no part in the story of Jesus. Less than four miles to the north lies Magdala. It was the native town of Mary Magdalene, the first person to whom Jesus appeared after his resurrection (John 20:11). Before Tiberias began to rival it, Magdala was doubtlessly the most important town by the lake, even though Josephus may have been exaggerating when he estimated the size of its population as 40,000. Its most important sources of income were weaving and fishing; salted fish from Magdala was in demand in distant marketplaces. Since the ancient town possessed a hippodrome, a certain part of the population must therefore have been non-Jewish — possibly Hellenistic. Originally it lay on the shores of the lake, but silting moved it inland. Today, no traces remain of its

Capernaum's synagogue was beautifully decorated with carvings of traditional Jewish religious symbols including palm-branches, pomegranates and citrons *(ethrog)*. The palm-tree (right), symbolic of fertility in the Middle East, was commonly represented in early churches and synagogues, as here at Capernaum.

former importance; only excavations could provide us with more exact information. To the north of it the hills recede and give way to the fertile plain of Gennesareth, which provides the lake with yet another name.

From Magdala the Lord frequently went to Bethsaida, which lay east of where the Jordan joined the lake in a large bay which has since been filled with sand, though lagoons remain a characteristic feature of this landscape today. Bethsaida was the capital of the tetrarch Philip, who built his seat on a rocky hill a couple of miles inland from the lake. The town was a center of the fishing industry, where according to the Talmud, 300 different kinds of fish were served in one dish. On the marshy ground by the Jordan, moorhens, which were considered a special delicacy, were caught. This was a very wealthy region — Zebedee must have had a thriving business with many day laborers (Mark 1:19). The economic life must have been detrimental to the religious life there, because Jesus called: "Woe to you, Chorazin! Woe to you, Bethsaida!" (Matthew 11:21). Nevertheless, the most important of the group of apostles came from just this

secularized region: Simon Peter, Andrew, Philip, and the sons of Zebedee, James and John.

To settle in, Jesus chose Capernaum (Kfar Nahum). Probably he lived in the house of Simon Peter; it became his second home and the center of his ministry. Here, he preached more often and performed more miracles than anywhere else. The question arises why Jesus should have chosen to settle in just this place; probably the position of the town helped to determine his choice. It was on the border between the territories of Herod Antipas and Philip. There was a customhouse there, with a garrison led by a centurion. The customhouse supervised the traffic on the lake. The many surviving black millstones and olive presses are evidence that the inhabitants were very industrious. Here Jesus encountered the most diverse types of people and his message aroused a far greater response than it would ever have done in Nazareth.

Several decisive events of Jesus' life took place in Capernaum. Here he healed the mother of Peter's wife of a fever (Matthew

"he went up on the mountain ...and taught them, saying: 'Blessed are the poor in spirit'" *(Matthew 5:1–3)*

On a high hill north of the Sea of Galilee, Jesus preached the "Sermon on the Mount." In commemoration, the Church of the Beatitudes, with a dome, was later built on the site. It overlooks the blue sea and the countryside sanctified by Jesus' words.

8:14), and at the request of the Roman centurion he healed that man's servant (Matthew 8:5–13). Here he raised from the dead the daughter of Jairus, the ruler of the synagogue, and healed the cripple. Especially this last action is very typical of his ministry: "And when he returned to Capernaum after some days, it was reported that he was at home. And many were gathered together, so that there was no longer room for them, not even about the door; and he was preaching the word to them. And they came, bringing to him a paralytic carried by four men. And when they could not get near him because of the crowd, they removed the roof above him; and when they had made an opening, they let down the pallet on which the paralytic lay. And when Jesus saw their faith, he said to the paralytic, 'My son, your sins are forgiven.' Now some of the scribes were sitting there, questioning in their hearts, 'Why does this man speak thus? It is blasphemy! Who can forgive sins but God alone?' And immediately Jesus, perceiving in his spirit that they thus questioned within themselves, said to them, 'Why do you question thus in your

"He (Jesus) ... taking the five loaves and the two fish h[e] ... gave the loaves to the disciples, and the disciples gave them t[o] ...

Two fishes and a basket of bread symbolize the miracle of the Multiplication of the loaves and fishes. The miracle took place, tradition says, at Tabgha (short for "Heptapegon," Greek for "Seven Springs"). The mosaic dates from the sixth century. Another detail from the mosaic floor (right): a peacock, symbolic of the immortality guaranteed by Christ.

hearts? Which is easier, to say to the paralytic, "Your sins are forgiven," or to say, "Rise, take up your pallet and walk"? But that you may know that the Son of man has authority on earth to forgive sins' — he said to the paralytic — 'I say to you, rise take up your pallet and go home.' And he rose, and immediately took up the pallet and went out before them all; so that they were all amazed and glorified God, saying, 'We never saw anything like this!'" (Mark 2:1–12).

The telling of the story is very graphic. Jesus returns "privately," so to speak, to Capernaum; but immediately the news spreads — he is at home; probably this means at the house of Peter. A crowd collects until there is no space left. When people want to bring the cripple to him they cannot force their way through. Without more ado they climb the outside staircase leading onto the roof, make an opening, and lower the sick man down until he comes to rest directly in front of Jesus. This extraordinary behavior, breaking all the generally accepted rules, shows how much confidence Jesus had already inspired. But the Lord does not wish to perform just one more

109

"...the kingdom of heaven is like a net which was thrown into the sea and gathered fish of every kind" (Matthew 13:47)

The so-called St. Peter's fish (*musht*) is the tastiest to be found in the Holy Land. In the miracle of the Multiplication, Jesus fed a large crowd with five loaves and two such fishes.

miracle. This is why he rather unexpectedly talks first about the remission of sins. This at once leads to a dispute with the Pharisees, who have come as passive but critical observers; to them, the saying of Jesus denies the divine order of things, because they consider that the remission of sins is the exclusive prerogative of God. To prove that his authority comes from God, Jesus speaks the words which heal the sick man; the effect at once silences all opposition, but it heightens the tension between Jesus and his enemies.

At the same time, the passage illustrates the vitality of Jewish religious life in Capernaum; it centered upon the synagogue, in which Jesus often delivered sermons; one of his most important sermons there was that concerning the bread of life: "'I am the bread of life; he who comes to me shall not hunger, and he who believes in me shall never thirst'" (John 6:35).

From the bread which satisfies physical hunger he turns to a different kind of bread, which he himself will provide.

While the town itself has been covered with centuries of soil, two holy buildings are still visible and command attention. The magnificent synagogue, which was reached by a flight of steps and contained three naves, is especially noteworthy because it is decorated ornamentally and symbolically with palm trees, foliage, fruit, geometrical designs, and also a representation of the Ark of the Covenant. It was built around the year 300, but it almost certainly replaces an older synagogue, in which Jesus must have preached.

There are chosen places in which revelations happen. Apart from mountains and hills there are also deep lakes surrounded by hills: it is no accident that there is a synagogue at the Sea of Galilee and that it was the scene of the ministry of Jesus. Not far from the synagogue is a Byzantine basilica with a baptistry and a magnificent mosaic representing a peacock, its body encircled by its colorful tail. Beneath it were found what must have been dwelling places of the very poor, one of which had been converted into a place of worship, above which the church was later erected. Graffiti in Hebrew, Greek, and Syriac script, expressing the usual invocations, indicate that this place has been venerated since ancient times and

This small church (left), not far from the Sea of Galilee, is in Migdal, ancient Magdala. This was the home of Mary Magdalene who had the courage to confess her sins and follow Jesus. Wheat harvesting in Galilee (right). Passing by such a wheat-field on the sabbath, Jesus permitted his disciples to pick a few ears and to eat the grains. Thus, by his own authority, Jesus broadened the narrow interpretation of biblical laws.

bear out the reports of early pilgrims, according to which the house of Simon Peter still existed in the first Christian centuries: "The house of the prince of the apostles has been converted into a church, the walls of which are still standing" (Aetheria, fourth century).

There is no other place on earth where the proximity of a synagogue and a church is of such profound religious significance as in Capernaum, where John says: "Simon Peter answered him, 'Lord, to whom shall we go? You have the words of eternal life; and we have believed, and have come to know, that you are the Holy One of God'" (John 6:68–69).

THE CHOICE OF THE APOSTLES

During this time, while crowds collected around Jesus from all sides, an important event took place: the choice of the apostles. For this Jesus prepared himself in conversation with God: "And he appointed twelve, to be with him, and to be sent out to preach and have authority to cast out demons: Simon whom he surnamed Peter; James the son of Zebedee and John the brother of James, whom

*"...Jesus went through the grainfields on the sabbath;
his disciples were hungry, and they began to pluck ears
of grain and to eat"* (Matthew 12:1)

In his travels, Jesus reached as far north as Caesarea Philippi, an area of lush vegetation where one of the sources of the Jordan flows (left). Niches cut in the rock (right) once housed idols of the Greek god Pan, whence the modern place-name Baniyas. Here, Peter acknowledged Jesus as the Messiah, In return, Jesus told him, "You are Peter, the rock, and on this rock I will build my church."

"When Jesus came into the district of Caesarea Philippi, he asked his disciples, 'Who do men say that the Son of man is?'" (Matthew 16:13)

he surnamed Boanerges, that is, sons of
thunder; Andrew, and Philip, and Bartholo-
mew, and Matthew, and Thomas, and James
the son of Alphaeus, and Thaddaeus, and
Simon the Cananaean, and Judas Iscariot,
who betrayed him" (Mark 3:14–19).

The idea of the apostles is connected with
the mission of the prophets, as Isaiah had
said: "The Spirit of the Lord God is upon me,
because the Lord has anointed me to bring
good tidings to the afflicted; he has sent me to
bind up the brokenhearted, to proclaim liberty
to the captives, and the opening of the prison
to those who are bound" (61:1).

But now the term is interpreted in a special,
a Christian sense, inasmuch as the apostles
are the legal, personal representatives of
Jesus: "'He who receives you receives me, and
he who receives me receives him who sent
me'" (Matthew 10:40).

The number twelve corresponds to the
twelve tribes of Israel; they will bear witness
to the transition from the old Israel to the
new. They are the constant companions of
Jesus, who initiates them into his secrets. Most
important of all, they witness his death and

116

"'Woe to you, Chorazin! woe to you, Bethsaida! for if the mighty works done in you had been done in Tyre and Sidon, they would have repented long ago in sackcloth and ashes'" (Matthew 11:21)

Some towns near the lakeshore of Galilee, like Chorazin and Bethsaida, refused to accept the teachings of Jesus and he cursed them.
The former site of Bethsaida (left). Ruins of the ancient synagogue of Chorazin (below).

his resurrection, which is the root of the Christian faith. Peter takes first place because he is destined to found the church. Judas, who will betray Jesus, comes last; coming from Judea, he is the only one who is not a Galilean. All these men were simple people, not Pharisees, scribes, or intellectuals. Jesus does not recognize social or cultural barriers between people; his only concern is that people be receptive to the word of God.

THE SERMON ON THE MOUNT

In villages and towns everywhere Jesus preached the new righteousness which is indeed based on the old conception of justice but acquires a new dynamic through the commandment that we must also love our enemies. On a mountainside not far from Capernaum, in the midst of a crowd of people, Jesus solemnly pronounces the Beatitudes:

"'Blessed are the poor in spirit, for theirs is the kingdom of heaven.

'Blessed are those who mourn, for they shall be comforted.

119

"...Jesus took with him Peter and James and John his brother, and led them up a high mountain apart"

(Matthew 17:1)

According to Byzantine tradition, Mount Tabor was the scene of Jesus' Transfiguration. The mountain is not named in the New Testament description of the event.

'Blessed are the meek, for they shall inherit the earth.

'Blessed are those who hunger and thirst for righteousness, for they shall be satisfied.

'Blessed are the merciful, for they shall obtain mercy.

'Blessed are the pure in heart, for they shall see God.

'Blessed are the peacemakers, for they shall be called sons of God.

'Blessed are those who are persecuted for righteousness' sake, for theirs is the kingdom of heaven.

'Blessed are you when men revile you and persecute you and utter all kinds of evil against you falsely on my account.

'Rejoice and be glad, for your reward is great in heaven, for so men persecuted the prophets who were before you'"

With the proclamation of the Beatitudes, the new order has been established. Now the kingdom of God alone means salvation; before it all worldly values are as nothing. And as surety for this new order stands he who has spoken these words, Jesus Christ. From ancient times, the attempt has been made to identify the place where the Sermon of the Mount was spoken. It is of little importance, because every hillside by the lake echoes with his words. But Aetheria, the woman pilgrim from Spain, mentioned a church built in commemoration of the event, the ruins of which can still be seen near Tabgha, and it is quite possible that Jesus preached there. Archaeological explorations have shown that the place was uninhabited until the Byzantines so that in the days of Jesus there was wild rock here; it is quite conceivable that a large crowd was able to collect without doing damage to cultivated land. The modern church, crowned with a cupola, stands on the summit of the hill; the view of the lake from there is indescribably beautiful. The panorama extends from the synagogue at Capernaum, visible through the trees, to the houses of Tiberias covering the hillside. This is the world in which Jesus preached and performed his miracles. Even if much that existed in those days has been lost to us forever, the landscape remains, reflecting

the glory of God. Above all, the powerful words remain, radiant upon the inner walls of the church and forever engraved on the minds of those who have once accepted them as true.

THE PLACE OF THE MULTIPLICATION

Tabgha — the name means seven springs — lies a short distance from Capernaum. The Church of the Multiplication, built in the Byzantine period, contains mosaics that are renowned throughout the world. The plants and animals are so alive that they might have come straight from the shores of the Sea of Galilee, and in the apse is a basket framed by two fishes, containing two loaves of bread, each marked with a cross. Beneath the altar is the holy stone mentioned by Aetheria as the one on which the Lord asked the loaves and fishes to be placed. In ancient times, artistic designs were rarely created by the efforts of one single individual but were the expression of a communal impulse. These magnificent representations testify that the multiplication, when about five thousand people were fed with five barley loaves and two small fishes (John

On the main altar in the upper Church of the Transfiguration, six candlesticks stand in line with the crucifix.

6:3–11), must have made an enormous impression on the early Christians.

History places the event on the eastern shore of the lake, but according to the ancient rules of worship, holy places tend to join together different events and so memory has transferred the story to Tabgha. The change only serves to emphasize that we are concerned here not with a simple miracle but with a religious manifestation of unique significance. It was a time of political and religious tension. John the Baptist had been executed— it was A.D. 29 — and Jesus could not afford to take the risk of going to celebrate the Passover in Jerusalem, where the Roman procurator Pilate had pilgrims from Galilee killed in the forecourt of the temple because he was afraid of a rebellion.

As this was a time of high Messianic expectation, it is not surprising that the crowd wished to make Jesus their Messianic king: "When the people saw the sign which he had done, they said 'This is indeed the prophet who is to come into the world'" (John 6:14). He had difficulties in getting away from the people.

"…he was transfigured… his face shone like the sun, and his garments became white as light" *(Matthew 17:2)*

The peak of Tabor has been revered for thousands of years. Beyond the latticed gateway can be seen the Syrian-style Latin Church of the Transfiguration erected in 1924 on ancient foundations. In the translucent mosaic (right), Jesus is shown transfigured, flanked by Moses and Elijah. His face became radiant and his garments turned white as snow.

BY THE POOL OF BETHZATHA

A little while later Jesus went to Jerusalem for "a feast of the Jews." This may well have been Shavuot or Pentecost, A.D. 29. There was a pool by the so-called sheep market near the present St. Stephen's Gate north of the temple area; its water was said to possess healing powers and so it was surrounded by a multitude of sick people. Here Jesus healed a cripple, commanding him: "'Rise, take up your pallet, and walk'" (John 5:8).

Some Pharisees saw the healed man carrying his bed and questioned Jesus, because it was a sabbath, a day on which it is not lawful to carry anything. Jesus answered them: "'My Father is working still, and I am working'" (John 5:17).

Their indignation became open hostility, because he had said that God was his father, and they wanted to kill him. The event was therefore a turning point in the life of Jesus. The place in which it occurred was of unique significance. Excavations have revealed the foundations of a Hellenistic-Roman thermal installation with two different basins which were once surrounded by five colonnades mentioned by John. There was no other similar installation, so this is one of the few places in Jerusalem of which we can say with absolute certainty that Jesus really stood here. During the Byzantine period, a church with three naves was built above the place; its imposing substructure remains. Beneath the northern aisle part of one of the basins has been preserved, in order to hold safe the memory of the miracle. Next to it have been found the remains of an old pagan place of worship, originally dedicated to a Semitic god and later to Asclepius, who was frequently worshiped near healing waters, as also in Tiberias and Gadara. Votive offerings from the second century — for instance, a foot dedicated by one Pompaia Lucilia — provide further evidence.

Here by the pool of Bethzatha we are faced with the interesting fact that pagan rites were probably still being practiced on the edge of the city, though outside its walls, in Jesus' time. It indicates that not by any means was all the population of Jerusalem orthodox, but there must also have been liberal groups, to one of which Herod himself must have belonged. Popular belief always exists as an undercurrent to the official religion; here it had gained the upper hand. Simple Jewish people imagined that an angel entered the pool and agitated the water and that this was how it acquired its healing powers; according to pagan belief it was Asclepius who healed people while they slept after having bathed. Jesus always went to find people in their own environment; to him Bethzatha was the place where illness and pain from all over the town congregated, and he intervened to alleviate them through his person and through his word.

THE PERSECUTED

A group of Pharisees and officials from the Sanhedrin went to Galilee to investigate "the case of Jesus." Their verdict was: His performance of miracles is a fact, but so is his disregard for the laws of the Torah. He does not keep the commandments concerning the sabbath or the purification rites or the fasts. And so he cannot be considered to be a prophet, his whole ministry must be based on deception, and he himself must be an assistant and a tool of the devils. The Torah is the measure of all things, and anyone who rebels against it is committing a heresy and makes himself liable to the most severe penalties, as is well known from Jewish writings: "He who offends knowingly and intentionally against the laws concerning the sabbath or against any other commandment of the Torah is impious. He must be warned and if he pays no heed and continues to violate the commandments of the Torah, he must be condemned to death and shall be stoned." Rebellion against the clergy in Jerusalem and defamation or desecration of the temple are punishable by death. Anyone who claims for himself divine honors or powers is impious. Anyone who knowingly blasphemes has to be arrested and may be convicted on the evidence of reliable witnesses. Anyone convicted of blasphemy must be stoned. After he has been stoned to death, his body shall be suspended from a tree. In the late afternoon on the day of the execution the body shall be taken from the tree and buried before dusk. A pseudo-prophet preaches abomination and tries to lead Israel to apostasy by means of dreams,

"Jacob's well was there, and so Jesus, wearied as he was with his journey, sat down beside the well" *(John 4:6)*

Returning to Galilee from Jerusalem, Jesus stopped in
Samaria at Jacob's well (left). There he asked a woman for
a drink and referred to himself as the source of water
valid for eternal life. Samaritans in their annual
Passover ceremony perform rites exactly as practiced in
the time of Jesus. The tiny sect has preserved
its own way of life around Mount Gerizim
for some two thousand five hundred years.

"As he drew near to Jericho, a blind man was sitting by the roadside begging... And he cried, 'Jesus, Son of David, have mercy on me!'" (Luke 18:35; 38)

visions, false prophecies, magic, conjuring up of the dead, hallucinations, and true miracles. He will most likely be considered a tool of the devil and must be tried by the Sanhedrin and if condemned must be executed in Jerusalem.

The situation had become threatening. As soon as he became suspect and the authorities began to show an interest in him, Jesus was deserted by many. But when he asked his twelve disciples whether they also wanted to leave him, Peter acknowledged in his answer the Messianic mission of Jesus (John 6:67—69). To avoid being declared outlawed, Capernaum also deserted him. It is typical of the close Oriental kinship ties that his family — probably Joseph was already dead — tried, though in vain, to save him by declaring that he was not responsible (Mark 3:21).

In Nazareth, a disturbance in the synagogue occurred when he interpreted the prophecy of Isaiah 61:1 as referring to himself and so proclaimed himself as the Messiah (Luke 4:29). His "arrogant" manner and the apparent lack of any substantiation of his claim increased the fury of his listeners so that they drove him out of the city and up a hill to throw him down

Jericho, a place of palms is thought to be the oldest city in the world. Here Jesus healed a blind man and visited the home of the publican Zacchaeus. In the foreground, archaeological excavations of a mound which is 10,000 years old.

from the height because of his blasphemy and, if necessary, afterward to stone him. This did not happen only because Jesus evaded them. The place of the event must have been one of the heights surrounding Nazareth. Luke failed to explain how Jesus evaded his persecutors, so popular imagination was given free rein. Already in the time of the Crusaders a hill about a mile and a half from the town was known as the Mount of the Precipitation, from which Jesus was said to have jumped across a deep wadi onto a cliff which was supposed to bear the imprint of his feet and garments. Beneath it was a cave, in which Mary was said to have hidden in fear. The memory is preserved by the modern chapel of Our Lady of the Fright, which is situated even closer to the town.

After this event, Jesus did not again return to Nazareth. He began to lead a restless existence: "'Foxes have holes, and birds of the air have nests; but the Son of man has nowhere to lay his head'" (Luke 9:58).

At first he remained in southern Galilee, where he again encountered the delegation from the Sanhedrin and was questioned by

The region of Jericho, with its reddish hills at the northern end of the Dead Sea, has always been a place of retreat for religiously minded people. At Qumran, evidence has been discovered of an ascetical Jewish sect living in Jesus' time.

132

them about the ritual washing of hands and the validity of the Torah (Matthew 15:1 — 4), and asked for a sign. The answers of Jesus became more and more pointed, and he warned his disciples to beware of agitators. He crossed for the first time the borders of the country, to Tyre and Sidon, in Phoenicia. Tyre possessed a magnificent necropolis and the right to strike its own coinage: the silver drachma from Tyre was valid in the temple! Jesus usually emphasized that he had been sent exclusively to the lost sheep of Israel — after his death the gospel was to conquer the world. Now he made a notable exception and healed the daughter of a woman of Canaan because she showed a great faith in him.

CAESAREA PHILIPPI

On the Day of Atonement, Jesus was in the neighborhood of Caesarea Philippi at the foot of Mount Hermon. Here is one of the three sources of the Jordan; welling up from a deep grotto dedicated to the god Pan, which gave the town its original name, Paneas. Today it is called Baniyas. Here Jesus asked the disciples who people thought the Son of man was, and

Approaching Jerusalem from the Jordan Valley and the east, travelers of old first viewed the Holy City from the top of the Mount of Olives. Jesus often looked down at Jerusalem from this vantage point.

*"...there is in Jerusalem by the Sheep Gate a pool,
in Hebrew called Bethzatha, which has five porticoes"*

(John 5:2)

The Pool of Bethzatha (left) lay not far from the
temple courtyard, but outside the city walls.
There, on a sabbath day, Jesus healed a paralytic.
Near the Pool is St. Anne's Church (right),
built by the Crusaders on a site
which one tradition holds was the
home of Joachim and Anne, Mary's parents.

Peter answered him: "'You are the Christ, the
Son of the living God'" (Matthew 16:16).

Then Jesus spoke the famous words: "'Blessed are you, Simon Bar-Jona! For flesh and
blood has not revealed this to you, but my
Father who is in heaven. And I tell you, you
are Peter, and on this rock I will build my
church, and the powers of death shall not prevail against it. I will give you the keys of the
kingdom of heaven, and whatever you bind on
earth shall be bound in heaven, and whatever
you loose on earth shall be loosed in heaven'".

This is the promise of the primacy, which all
Peter's successors shall inherit from him. As
Abraham is the rock upon which God built the
world, so Peter is the foundation upon which
Jesus builds his church, which is indeed a new
edifice and not a special branch of the ancient
people. The bunch of keys is the sign of the
steward, who is the representative of the Lord
himself. The image is one taken from everyday
life: Palestine is a country of keys; the Church
of the Holy Sepulchre is still locked and un-
locked with ceremonious solemnity even today,
and the door of the synagogue of the Samaritans bears three separate locks, the keys to

137

"'Go, wash in the pool of Siloam' ... he went and washed and came back seeing" *(John 9:7)*

Another famous pool in Jerusalem is the pool of Siloam. There Jesus sent a man, blind from birth, to wash in the waters. The invalid's eyes became normal, and for the first time he saw himself reflected in the water.

which are in the hands of three different stewards.

The promise indicates the sphere of the church. Not far from Caesarea is the second source of the Jordan, Dan, used in the phrase "from Dan to Beersheba" as the most northerly point in the land of Canaan. An imposing gateway and a citadel dating from the time of the kingdom of Israel as well as Roman remains have been found there; although Dan is not mentioned in the New Testament, it is likely that Jesus visited the place. The proximity of Dan to Caesarea Philippi — whether chance or design — shows in its own way that Christianity was a new experience. Jesus now turned away from the multitude and concentrated entirely on teaching his disciples and preparing them for the difficult events before them: "From that time Jesus began to show his disciples that he must go to Jerusalem and suffer many things from the elders and chief priests and scribes, and be killed, and on the third day be raised" (Matthew 16:21).

ON MOUNT TABOR

A week later, Jesus ascended a high mountain

together with the most faithful of his disciples,
Peter, James, and John, who were soon to ac-
company him to Gethsemane. Perhaps this
was Mount Hermon; possibly it was, as Byzantine tradition suggests, Mount Tabor,
which stands isolated in the midst of a plain;
it may have been another mountain — we
cannot be sure. They received a revelation of
the glory of the Messiah, so that they might
remember it while awaiting the resurrection of
the Son of man.

The experience was a unique epiphany:
"And he was transfigured before them, and
his face shone like the sun, and his garments
became white as light. And behold, there appeared to them Moses and Elijah, talking with
him. And Peter said to Jesus, 'Lord, it is well
that we are here; if you wish, I will make three
booths here, one for you and one for Moses
and one for Elijah.' He was still speaking,
when lo, a bright cloud overshadowed them,
and a voice from the cloud said, 'This is my
beloved Son, with whom I am well pleased;
listen to him'" (Matthew 17:2 — 5).
A modern church on Mount Tabor, built in

Syrian style upon the ruins of a Crusaders'
church, reflects the magnificent mystery which
it commemorates in its mosaics and chapels,
but above all in the play of light when the sunshine penetrates the interior. The view is
unique; it is impossible to describe the effect
upon it of dawn or dusk, of the sun rising in
the east or setting in a blood-red western sky.
The panorama extends across the whole of
Galilee, from the hills of Samaria to Mount
Hermon and the town on the hill, from the
Carmel range to the Sea of Galilee, the water
of which flashes mysteriously when it is touched by the rays of the rising sun. Among the
many hamlets and villages, Nain deserves to be
mentioned; here Jesus brought back to life
the only son of a widow (Luke 7:11).

AT THE FEAST OF TABERNACLES

Jesus was very fond of the liturgy. During the
Feast of Tabernacles, A.D. 29, the situation was
very tense. People were talking about him;
opinion was divided. While the priests carrying
willow branches moved in procession seven
times around the altar of the burnt offering
and the high priest sprinkled water from the

"Now a certain man was ill, Lazarus of Bethany, the village of Mary and her sister Martha" *(John 11:1)*

Jesus often visited Bethany near Jerusalem (right). Here he restored to life his friend Lazarus who had been dead for some days. The Arabic name of the locality is still El-'Azariyeh. Nuns in white veils (left) visit the Church of Lazarus in Bethany.

pool of Siloam, Jesus exclaimed in a loud voice: "' If any one thirst, let him come to me and drink. He who believes in me, as the scripture has said, "Out of his heart shall flow rivers of living water"'" (John 7:37 — 38).

Probably it was during a time when the temple was festively illuminated that he spoke the words: "' I am the light of the world; he who follows me will not walk in darkness, but will have the light of life'" (John 8:12).

It was during these days that the events took place which are related in the story of the woman taken in adultery, whom Jesus pardoned, having been empowered by God to do so (John 8:6 — 11). Jesus excited the greatest attention. The police were sent to arrest him "but no one laid hands on him." And when the high priests asked the officers why they did not carry out their orders, the answer was: "'No man ever spoke like this man'" (John 7:44,46).

BY THE POOL OF SILOAM

We are standing by the pool of Siloam, to the south of Jerusalem in the Valley of the Cheesemakers. Around us are flowering terraces and orchards; here were once the gardens of Solomon. On the ground lie pieces of broken columns from times past. Arab women are washing clothes, children play in the water; a bucolic idyll. Especially on Fridays, one may occasionally observe men and women in the shadow of minaret solemnly and ceremoniously pouring water over themselves seven times in order to be healed of some sickness.

The Moslems still tend to recognize the pool as a holy place, as the Christians once did. Jews visit here today at the Feast of Tabernacles. Not far from here, Jesus healed a blind man and then, to test his faith, sent him to wash himself at the pool. The authorities instituted an investigation; the man whom Jesus had healed was summoned. That it was indeed a cure was confirmed; but again Jesus had violated the sabbath laws, and therefore they would not admit that he had worked a miracle but charged him with blasphemy. And all those who believed in him were themselves punishable. The authorities wanted to issue a warning to others, and so the healed man was publicly cast out of the community. He was

"When he (Jesus) had said this, he cried with a loud voice, 'Lazarus, come out '" *(John 11:43)*

The flight of stairs leading down to the tomb of Lazarus. The grave was carved out of the rock of the hillside.

"Jesus said to her, 'I am the resurrection and the life'"

The Church of Lazarus, Bethany, in its lower half, recalls Lazarus lying in the tomb and Jesus' promise: "I am the resurrection and the life."

forbidden to have any business or social relations with other people. The struggle between Jesus and his enemies was nearing its climax. Jesus revealed himself as the Son of man to the man whom he had healed — an ordinary man, who acknowledged him (John 9:1 — 39).

THE SHEPHERD

In December, during the Feast of the Dedication of the Temple, Jesus was walking in Solomon's Porch when he was asked if he were the Messiah: "Jesus answered them, 'I told you, and you do not believe. The works that I do in my Father's name, they bear witness to me; but you do not believe, because you do not belong to my sheep. My sheep hear my voice, and I know them, and they follow me; and I give them eternal life, and they shall never perish, and no one shall snatch them out of my hand. My Father, who has given them to me, is greater than all, and no one is able to snatch them out of the Father's hand. I and the Father are one'" (John 10:25 — 30).

When he had finished speaking they threw

The village of Bethany lies at the foot of the Mount of Olives. For thousands of years, the inhabitants of the place have been engaged in the production of olive oil. This press (left) dates from the Middle Ages but in Jesus' time much the same technique was used. Bethany, old and new (right); the ruins of a Crusader tower and a modern Greek Orthodox Church.

148

"And seeing a fig tree ... (Jesus) found nothing on it but leaves only. And he said to it, 'May no fruit ever come from you again'" (Matthew 21:19)

stones at him, not because he had said he was the Messiah but because they considered that he had blasphemed by saying that he himself was God. The good shepherd, the way in which Christian art first pictured Jesus, is not an idyllic image, as is proved by its relevance to the final struggle of Jesus. It symbolizes the choice of a duality: he is strong and valiant in his fight to defend his position against all his opponents, but charitable and tender toward those in his care. Jesus evaded his enemies and returned to the place from which he had once set out. On the banks of the river Jordan, where he was baptized, he preached and had many followers: "He went away again across the Jordan to the place where John at first baptized, and there he remained" (John 10:40).

IN BETHANY

Bethany lies on the southeastern slope of the Mount of Olives, on the edge of the desert. It was isolated and peaceful — not yet crossed by the modern road to Jericho — and it was one of Jesus' favorite places. On his walks across the Mount of Olives he often called at the house of Lazarus, where Mary and Martha lived. The

In this neighborhood another of Jesus' miracles occurred. He cursed a fig tree, full of springtime growth, and all its leaves withered away.

evangelists describe three of his visits there. It became known all over the world because of the raising of Lazarus, after whom the present Arab village El-'Azariyeh is named. The brother had died and the sisters sent for Jesus. His disciples tried to dissuade him from going into a district where his life was threatened, but he insisted, and Thomas, the twin, was the first to say that they all ought to share his fate: "'Let us also go, that we may die with him'" (John 11:16).

The passage in John is so graphic and tender that anyone who reads it must be deeply moved. When they arrived, Lazarus was dead and had already been buried; there was a crowd of mourners. Outside the village, Jesus and his disciples met Martha and in the conversation which followed, this simple woman became inspired. In the midst of her grief she recognized the light in Jesus: "'Yes, Lord; I believe that you are the Christ, the Son of God, he who is coming into the world'" (John 11:27).

Mary joined them; she was weeping so much that she could not speak. Together they went to the graveside. Jesus himself was deeply moved and wept. He requested that the stone be removed, said a prayer of thanks to God, and called with a loud voice: "'Lazarus, come out.' The dead man came out, his hands and feet bound with bandages, and his face wrapped with a cloth. Jesus said to them, 'Unbind him, and let him go'" (John 11:43—44).

The tomb was a typical one, cut out of the rock, containing an antechamber and a burial chamber in which the dead lay on a slab of rock. The modern church in the vicinity is built like a mausoleum; its mosaics symbolize the words spoken by Jesus to Martha: "'I am the resurrection and the life; he who believes in me, though he die, yet shall he live, and whoever lives and believes in me shall never die'" (John 11:25—26). These words are spoken at every Christian funeral.

THE WARRANT FOR ARREST

The raising of Lazarus had serious consequences for Jesus. The rabbis considered that the raising of the dead involved the practice of magic or conjuring. A special meeting of the Sanhedrin was called. The members were confronted with a dilemma: on the one hand, the people had been tremendously impressed by the miracle; on the other, there was the danger that the Romans would intervene if the Messianic movement should spread: "'If we let him go on thus, every one will believe in him, and the Romans will come and destroy both our holy place and our nation'" (John 11:48).

The acting high priest, Caiaphas, urged them to reach a decision: "'You know nothing at all; you do not understand that it is expedient for you that one man should die for the people, and that the whole nation should not perish...' So from that day on they took counsel how to put him to death" (John 11:49—53).

For forty days a herald was made to proclaim to the population that anyone knowing the whereabouts of Jesus should at once notify the police so that he might be arrested (John 11:57; Sanhedrin 43a). This happened during February, A.D. 30. Jesus did not at once give himself up to the police but evaded capture because he wanted to meet his death as the paschal lamb at the time of the Passover. He tarried at first in Ephraim, the present Et-

Taijibe, which lies rather isolated in the hills about twelve miles from Jerusalem, in the midst of fertile olive groves with a magnificent view of the Judean Desert and the Jordan Valley. Probably Jesus had been there many times before. The ruins of the Byzantine church with its baptismal font and lighted candles and the generally Christian atmosphere of the village with its three churches indicate that this was a place with which Jesus was closely associated.

In the week before Passover, Jesus moved down to Jericho. He passed the site of the ancient fortified Jericho, which was destroyed by Joshua. At that time, the remains were buried within a hill, which has been investigated by modern excavations. New Jericho extended south of it across the plain, as had been described by the ancient writer Strabo: "covering it with dwellings and an abundance of fruit trees and palms." The ample spring which the prophet Elisha had turned from brackish to sweet drinking water was guided through channels to make fields and gardens fertile. This was the site of Herod's winter palace, and many rich citizens lived here in

"And he said to them, 'When you pray, say: Father, hallowed be thy name. Thy kingdom come'" (Luke 11:2)

On the Mount of Olives, Jesus taught his disciples many things including the Lord's Prayer. To commemorate his role as teacher, the church and monastery of "Pater Noster" were erected. In the cloister (left), the prayer is written in forty-four languages. In Norwegian and Aramaic (below).

"'I am the vine, you are the branches. He who abides in me, and I in him, he it is that bears much fruit...'"

(John 15:5)

In Jerusalem Jesus spoke the parable of the vine. In olden times, there were many vineyards and wine presses in the Holy Land. The vine is thus a frequent symbol in the Bible.

houses decorated with mosaics, among them the tax collector Zacchaeus, whose home Jesus visited (Luke 19:1 — 10). As he was leaving the town he was greeted as the Messiah by a blind man who called him "Jesus, Son of David" (Mark 10:47), and Jesus healed him.

On purpose, Jesus chose the route which ascends from the Jordan Valley to Jerusalem. By the Jordan River, which marked the boundary of the Promised Land, he had begun his ministry, which was about to reach its climax in the Passion. He was joined by many pilgrims as he climbed the Roman road through the Wadi Kelt, past where the Greek monastery Choziba today clings to the cliff face. It was founded during the Byzantine period in honor of Mary. The wild ravines and the heights of bright red rock looking in places as if it were covered with blood are the setting of the parable of the good Samaritan and also of the words of the Lord describing this journey: "'Behold, we are going up to Jerusalem; and the Son of man will be delivered to the chief priests and the scribes, and they will condemn him to death, and deliver him to the Gentiles; and they will mock him, and spit upon him,

"...'Go into the village opposite, where on entering you will find a colt tied... untie it and bring it here'"

(Luke 19:30)

From the village of Bethpage (left) Jesus rode on an ass to a triumphal welcome in Jerusalem. This Gospel event is commemorated each year by the Latin Church's Palm Sunday procession. A fresco in Bethpage chapel (right) depicts the Gospel story.

and scourge him, and kill him; and after three days he will rise'" (Mark 10:33—34).

In Bethany, Mary, the sister of Lazarus, humbly anointed his feet as he sat at supper, which caused Judas to make the tactless remark that the money might have been better used for the poor. The evangelist comments: "This he said, not that he cared for the poor but because he was a thief, and as he had the money box he used to take what was put into it" (John 12:6).

PALM SUNDAY

Jesus climbed the Mount of Olives, the place of revelation. According to Ezekiel, here the glory of God would be made manifest (11:23), and Zechariah prophesied that the feet of God would stand upon it during a tremendous epiphany (14:4). Expecting that he would intervene on their behalf in politics, the pilgrims came out of the town with palm branches and shouts of hosanna to meet the Messiah and to escort him in a solemn procession. Jesus allowed them to lead him. But somewhere near Bethpage, on the slopes of the Mount of Olives, he got onto an ass and thus

gave them to understand that he was not a heroic warrior entering his capital on a charger but the Prince of Peace, bringing salvation with gentleness and humility and not with battle cries and the force of weapons. Within the chapel of Bethpage there is a rock, preserving this scene forever in frescoes dating from the times of the Crusaders, and the traditional liturgical procession on Palm Sunday has engraved it ineradicably in the hearts of the faithful. Of special interest is the mention of Galileans on the lid of an ossuary found at Bethpage which may shed some light on the ease with which the apostles were able to procure the ass for the triumphal entry of Jesus. Bethpage had been a Galilean settlement, and we can suppose that also the family of Lazarus at Bethany was of Galilean origin. Here Jesus joined compatriots.

When Jesus reached the summit of the Mount of Olives and saw before him the temple and the towers within the walls of the city, all radiant in the sunshine, he "wept over it, saying, 'Would that even today you knew the things that make for peace! But now they are

160

"when he drew near and saw the city he wept over it"
(Luke 19:41)

hid from your eyes. For the days shall come upon you, when your enemies will cast up a bank about you and surround you, and hem you in on every side, and dash you to the ground, you and your children within you, and they will not leave one stone upon another in you; because you did not know the time of your visitation'" (Luke 19:41 — 44).

The words contrast strangely with the rejoicings of the surrounding crowd, yet no one who is familiar with the many contradictions inherent in this country and its people will be surprised! Not far from there, the scene is commemorated by the small chapel of Dominus Flevit. It is one of the most beautiful sites in the vicinity of Jerusalem. The view extends across the deep Valley of Kidron to the Temple Mount and the Aqsa Mosque. Beyond it one can see the black cupola of the Church of the Holy Sepulchre and the modern tower of the Lutheran Church of the Redeemer. The Dormition Abbey is quite clearly visible. The whole city nestles among the rolling hills, stretching from Ramat Rachel to the Tomb of Samuel. And the height itself which grants this view bears traces of many bygone centuries: the ancient Tombs of the Jebusites, which contained a scarabaeus of the Egyptian Pharaoh Thutmose III, who reigned more than a thousand years before Christ, and Jewish family tombs from the time of Jesus. There are also remains of a Byzantine church and convent which were decorated with mosaics. A chapel recently built upon the ancient ruins provides an example of modern Italian church architecture; its wrought-iron windows recall the mystery of the Christian faith with a representation of the cup and the crown of thorns. In this place the deeper meaning of the "visitation" of which Jesus speaks suddenly becomes clear. It is not merely a judgment bringing total destruction; it is also a blessing which allows new life to grow out of the ruins.

Jesus must have followed the ancient Roman road, which leads from Jericho across the ridge of the Mount of Olives, first down into the valley and from there up to the city; it is no longer possible to trace the actual road. In the ninth century, a tradition arose that Jesus entered the temple area through the Golden Gate, in ancient times reserved for the priests.

him shouted, 'Hosanna to the Son of David!...Hosanna...'"

(Matthew 21:9)

Nuns carry the *lulav* (palm frond) and sing "Hosanna to
the Son of David" (left). This annual procession marks
the beginning of the Holy Week for the Latin Church.
The procession crosses the Kidron valley and enters the
walls of Jerusalem through St. Stephen's Gate,
ending in the courtyard of St. Anne's Church (below).

The Sultan Suleiman ordered it to be walled up, so that no one should pass that way until the return of Christ. The jubilation of the pilgrims long ago is echoed by the sound of the children who line the route of the procession in our own day. In the Middle East, people compare the stammering of a child with the speech of a prophet, and the stuttering with that of a saint.

During the next few days Jesus went to the temple daily to heal the sick and to preach. To his enemies he was a thorn in the flesh. However, they did not dare to arrest him among the crowds of pilgrims and so they endeavored to involve him in all sorts of controversies in order to expose him — as, for instance, when they asked him whether or not taxes ought to be paid to the emperor. Jesus was too intelligent to allow them to compromise him. Soon afterward the chief priests, the scribes, and the elders assembled in the house of the acting high priest, Caiaphas, to discuss their plans, and they decided to catch Jesus by means of a trick in order not to cause a public disturbance, and then to kill him (Matthew 26:3 ff.). Judas, who had probably been acting as an informer on Jesus and his disciples for some time, offered his services for thirty pieces of silver. The tragic figure of this man can be understood only within the obscure framework of destiny surrounding all human beings.

THE LAST SUPPER

The festival of Passover with its Seder celebration was approaching. In antiquity, the observance of the holy days played such an important part that several different calendars were in use, as there are among Christians even today. The date of Passover varied; according to John and the sources from Qumran, it seems that Jesus celebrated the festival with his disciples a few days before the "official" date. The house in which this celebration took place is not known. It may have been anywhere among the maze of streets in the Old City. The name of their host is also unknown, which is not surprising in a country which places such emphasis on hospitality and where especially on the Seder night all families open their doors to pilgrims and strangers. The hall shown today as the place of the Last Supper, built in the Gothic style by Franciscans in the fourteenth century, is the place where the the early Christian community used to assemble before Pentecost. Thus in this place the later and the earlier events have been joined together. Is not the obscurity surrounding this place a reflection of that holy night from which the light of Christ emanates in a very special way?

Jesus, whose faith was firmly rooted in the religious traditions of his people, celebrated a true Seder, which acquired another meaning, emphasized by the evangelists, through the personality of Jesus. Before beginning, the head of the family washes his hands. The evangelists do not mention it, but it is likely that there followed the telling of the story of the exodus of the Children of Israel from Egypt, proceeding through spontaneous questions and answers between the head of the family and the youngest person present — which was probably John. The bitter herbs, the bread of affliction, and above all, his imminent betrayal by Judas provided Jesus with the occasion to allude to his Passion: "'Truly, truly, I say to you, one of you will betray me... It is he to whom I shall give this morsel when

I have dipped it.' So when he had dipped the morsel, he gave it to Judas, the son of Simon Iscariot" (John 13:21, 26).

According to ancient custom, the head of the family offers the first mouthful to one of those present as a sign of their specially close relationship. That is the great tragedy, that this gesture became here an indication of the division between them; Jesus offered the bitter herbs to the one who would betray him, who afterward left the table. Next the Lord took, as the sequence of the Seder demands, the unleavened bread, symbolizing in the old tradition the people of Israel, and spoke the decisive new words: "'Take, eat; this is my body.'"

When the cup of grace was passed, he said: "'Drink of it, all of you; for this is my blood of the covenant, which is poured out for many...'" (Matthew 26:27 — 28).

The celebration had been transformed by the fact that Jesus offered himself to the disciples; the theme of remembrance which had dominated the Seder acquired a deeper meaning through the eternal presence of Jesus, and the blood which was spilled would become the

167

salvation of the whole of mankind. After the meal, they remained together in serious conversation, and Jesus talked especially about the close relationship between the master and his disciples, in the parable of the true vine: "'I am the vine, you are the branches. He who abides in me, and I in him, he it is that bears much fruit, for apart from me you can do nothing.... If you abide in me, and my words abide in you, ask whatever you will, and it shall be done for you'" (John 15:5, 7).

They all had the feeling that this was a leavetaking. After praying to his Father in Heaven, he rose from the table and went with his disciples through the Valley of Kidron to Gethsemane, as they had to remain in Jerusalem because it was Passover.

GETHSEMANE

There was an estate there with an olive grove and an oil press; probably it belonged to one of Jesus' friends. The night of the Seder is the *Leil Shimurim,* the night of the watchers, in which God once determinedly saved his people, who have been since commanded always to keep watch during the late hours.

On Mount Zion three religions meet. The tomb of David is sacred to Jews and Moslems. In the same precincts was the scene of Jesus' Last Supper.

168

"'The Teacher says..., Where is the guest room, where I am to eat the passover with my disciples?'" *(Luke 22:11)*

Jesus took with him only his closest friends, Peter, James, and John, and asked them to keep watch while he prayed. A stone's throw away he knelt down. Out of the terrible loneliness of a human being he pleaded with his Father in Heaven: "'Abba, Father, all things are possible to thee; remove this cup from me.'"

But as during the whole of his Messianic ministry, he submitted to the will of God even at this moment: "'Yet not what I will, but what thou wilt'" (Mark 14:36).

He stood up and went to find comfort among his friends, only to discover that they had fallen asleep. He asked Peter: "'Could you not watch one hour? Watch and pray that you may not enter into temptation'" (Mark 14:37—38).

While he was talking to his disciples, he was perhaps referring to himself; in his fear of death he sweated blood as a token of the blood which he would before long shed on the cross. But this was the night of *Leil Shimurim:* his Father in Heaven sent him an angel to comfort him. His blood was not to be shed in vain, but would serve to redeem others.

The Cenacle (in Latin *Coenaculum:* "Dining Room") is in the upper floor of this building. Here Jesus and his disciples ate the Last Supper.

170

"And he will show you a large ... room furnished; there make ready"

(Luke 22:12)

In this large room, the Last Supper was taken, according to old belief. One Byzantine column still stands in the Crusader reconstruction. The slender pillar in the left-rear corner bears a medieval capital with the Pelican-Christ motif.

Meanwhile, the detachment coming to arrest him drew nearer: Roman soldiers with swords, the Jewish guardians of the temple with clubs and staves, led by Judas. He greeted Jesus in front of the grotto with a kiss, as is customary in the Middle East, and in this way identified him to the others. Jesus allowed himself to be arrested and led away, without offering resistance; but his disciples abandoned him and took flight.

In the Garden of Gethsemane there are eight very ancient olive trees; they are at least one thousand years old. They look as if they were petrified, and yet fresh young shoots continue to sprout from them — a true symbol of the *Leil Shimurim*! They cast their shade on the Basilica of the Agony, which rests upon the foundations of a church built by Byzantines and the Crusaders; the windows of a bluish alabaster veil the interior with a half-light. Through them one can see the naked rock on which Jesus is said to have prayed.

THE TRIAL OF JESUS

The legal proceedings were among the shortest in world history, and also among the most

172

"And they led Jesus to the high priest..." (Mark 14:53)

By this road Jesus descended from Mount Zion, across the Kidron Valley to Gethsemane. Remains of the ancient stepped road dating from Maccabean times can still be seen near the Church of St. Peter in Gallicantu (Cockcrow) commemorating Peter's repentance after the triple denial of his Master.

momentous. The detailed reports in the Gospels indicate the importance of the trial and also its authenticity. We remain uncertain about a number of details that happened during its course, because out of the abundance of the material which must have been available, each of the evangelists selected the particulars that seemed to him to illuminate best the personality of Jesus. And so we can arrive only at uncertain conclusions about a number of problems, of which we will examine a few.

THE DATE OF THE TRIAL

Jesus was crucified on a Friday in the year 30, so his public ministry must have lasted at least two years. John explicitly testifies that it happened on the day before Passover. Mark, Matthew, and Luke give the impression that the trial took place in extreme haste within the space of one day, on which sittings were held early and late. But it has to be remembered that the writers of these summaries were not particularly interested in the several phases of the trial, but only in its outcome, the death of their Lord. Jesus may have celebrated the

From the Grotto of the Betrayal
Jesus went out to meet his captors.
Restored to something like its
original form, it still shows inscriptions
dating from the twelfth century.

The Basilica of the Agony was built in
1924 on Byzantine and Crusader
remains. The mosaic represents
Christ's offering up to his Father his
sufferings and those of the world.

"...*he said to his disciples, 'Sit here, while I go yonder and pray'*"

(Matthew 26:36)

Twelve domes in the ceiling of the Basilica of the Agony and other ornaments in the church recall the names of sixteen generous nations, hence its modern name "Church of All Nations."

178

The rock of the Agony (below) is thought to be where Jesus sweated blood before being led prisoner from the Garden up to Jerusalem. The might of ancient Jerusalem is still recalled by its walls, here pierced by St. Stephen's Gate (right).

Passover meal according to some other calendar, perhaps on Tuesday, which would leave at least two full days for the trial if John was referring to the Passover according to the official reckoning used in the temple. In this uncertainty, we are confronted with the eastern mentality with its various systems of calculating time. Even at present, many different calendars are in use: the Jewish, the Moslem and the Christian which itself takes different forms: the Latin, the Greek Orthodox, the Coptic etc. This is a result of reckoning the phases according to personal observations.

The problem which still concerns people very much today is the question of who was responsible for the decision to condemn Jesus to death. The Jewish religious supreme court, the Sanhedrin, carried out an official preliminary investigation; probably it did not in fact pass a death sentence but instead reached the conclusion to hand Jesus over to Pilate and to accuse him of a crime which carried the death penalty, which would be the reason why the procurator himself had to take charge of the hearing. The accusation relied on the claim

"...the soldiers plaited a crown of thorns, and put it on his head, and arrayed him a purple robe" *(John 19:2)*

During his trial, Jesus was crowned with thorns. Christians view such a crown as symbolic, as is evident in the dome of the shrine of "The Flagellation" (left). A variety of rugged thorns (right) is still to be seen in Holy Land flora.

"and they bound him and led him away and delivered him to Pilate the governor"

(*Matthew 27:2*)

A dome topped by a cross stands over the traditional site of Lithostratos, the flagstone courtyard of the Roman fortress Antonia. Here Jesus is said to have been tried by the Roman governor, Pontius Pilate.

"Then he handed him over to them to be crucified"

(John 19:16)

After Jesus was scourged, Pilate had him led out in full view of the watching crowd and said, "Ecce Homo" — "Here is the man." The archway (below) in the interior of the Basilica "Ecce Homo" is prolonged outside in the Via Dolorosa by a similar arch, which bears the name "Ecce Homo" today. Sisters of Zion in prayer in the Basilica (right). Behind the altar the Roman archway frames the apse.

Jesus had made that he was the Messiah, which was interpreted as blasphemy and at the same time concealed political implications. The Romans were suspicious of all messianic movements, and therefore a suggestion of them brought the danger that the army of occupation might interfere with Jewish privileges. While emphasis was placed on the religious aspect of the charge when it was put before the Sanhedrin and before Pilate, the political aspect of it was important. It ought to be remembered that both sides indubitably worked together.

In recent times the suggestion has been made that the trial should be reviewed, to see if it is possible to discover certain legal shortcomings. Apart from the fact that renewed proceedings cannot be undertaken because no official documents exist, judging by what we know of the law of that time we have no reason to find fault with the trial from a legal point of view. For any religious person, these questions are of minor importance. The trial of Jesus is an example of how, in the midst of the chaos created by human insufficiency and frailty, God's intentions are fulfilled: "'Was it

not necessary that the Christ should suffer these things and enter into his glory?'" (Luke 24:26).

Jesus is the suffering servant of God, whose coming the prophet Isaiah had foretold.

THE GUILT OF THE DEATH OF JESUS

During his public ministry, Jesus had many disputes with the Pharisees. During the trial, the opposition of the Sadducees became more important. They were officially in charge of the temple and were concerned with maintaining a good relationship between themselves and the Romans. But all the parties were represented at the decisive sitting of the Sanhedrin, and so none of them can be absolved from responsibility. As everywhere, there were a few opportunists among them; but most of them were driven by the zeal to do God's work as they understood it. This zeal, from which the Zealots took their name, is characteristic of the Middle East and can easily degenerate into fanaticism. At first, the people supported Jesus enthusiastically; later they demanded his death from Pilate. They were suffering from a psychosis that may still be observed occasionally in the Middle East today. In this connection, we ought to remember a saying quoted only by Matthew; it is almost proverbial, and Matthew accorded much significance to it: "'His blood be on us and on our children'" (27:25).

Pilate was an average Roman procurator; he was concerned about his career, and as chief of the army of occupation he was carrying on a sort of "cold war" against the Jewish leaders. He was an anti-Semite and never pretended to be anything else. He was honest enough to see that Jesus was not a criminal, but on the other hand he was not strong enough to rally effectively to his defense. He was basically contemptuous of people and attached no importance to human life. Jesus was for him only an episode, which he may well have forgotten overnight. Herod Antipas, governor of Galilee and so the sovereign of Jesus, who had come as a pilgrim to the festival in Jerusalem, may also have been active behind the scenes, although the Gospels do not make this clear. Jesus once called him "a fox," and the Pharisees report that he wanted to kill Jesus: "'Get away from here, for Herod wants to kill you'" (Luke 13:31 — 32).

In the final analysis, all those who had anything to do with the trial must share the guilt. But perhaps a distinction ought to be made between active guilt and passive guilt which only God can judge. We must be guided by the words spoken by Jesus as he was dying: "'Father, forgive them; for they know not what they do'" (Luke 23:34).

THE LOCATION OF THE TRIAL

The Sanhedrin may have sat in the house of Caiaphas or possibly in the great portico on the Temple Mount. According to ancient tradition, the proceedings before Pilate took place in the fortress of Antonia, part of the barracks on the northern side of the temple area, the remains of which are still visible today. Nowadays people are inclined to think that it must have occurred in Herod's former palace by the Jaffa Gate, where the procurator used to live when he came to Jerusalem from his official residence in Caesarea. This high-lying citadel provided a good view of the whole city. In front of it was a paved square, officially called Lithostratos, where Pilate dispensed justice.

This was where the way of the cross began; it is not possible to reconstruct the route exactly. Anyone who had been declared guilty was led for a short while through the busiest streets as an example to others. It is necessary to make a distinction between the historically possible way of the cross and that accepted by religion, which is based on an old tradition of the Crusaders and made meaningful by the prayers of millions of religious people. Devout believers hold a weekly procession along the Stations of the Cross and so continually re-animate the tradition. The temple area itself is not linked to the Christian religion by any memory of Jesus, because it was considered desecrated after its destruction by the Romans.

JESUS BEFORE ANNAS

After his arrest on the evening of the Last Supper, Jesus was led through the Valley of Kidron, past the tombs of Zachariah, Hezir, and Absalom, up the steps — still visible today — to the city above, to the district near the Dormition Abbey where the wealthier part of

There are many caves to the east of Lithostratos and along the Way of the Cross (Via Dolorosa). The Greek Orthodox community points out one as the prison of Christ or perhaps of Barabbas.

the population was living. He was taken into the house of Caiaphas, now commemorated by an Armenian chapel, on Mount Zion, where distinguished and aristocratic people once dwelt. According to true Oriental tradition he was first of all introduced to Annas, the father-in-law of the high priest and the head of the family. The beginning of the investigation, therefore, was not undertaken officially. Annas questioned him, perhaps in the presence of others, about his doctrine and his disciples. Jesus answered: 'Why do you ask me? Ask those who have heard me, what I said to them'.

One of the servants hit Jesus in the face and Jesus protested. He spent the night in that house, and it was in its courtyard that Peter denied him before the servants and thus fulfilled the prophecy of Jesus that he would do so before the crowing of the cock, a fair indication of the time, because the period from midnight to 3 a.m. is the time of the "cock-crowing." This later became a symbol of penitence in Christian imagery. Peter left and wept by the wall. The Church of St. Peter in Gallicantu (cockcrow) commemorates this event.

JESUS BEFORE THE SANHEDRIN

In the morning, Jesus was probably brought to the great portico to appear before the Sanhedrin, which had meanwhile been summoned. The Sanhedrin was the highest religious authority in the land, drawing its members from three different groups: the high priests; the elders of the people, mostly influential landowners, that is, laymen; and scribes, that is, Pharisees. The assembly was presided over by Caiaphas; it is not known whether he was wearing the official robes of his office. They sat in a half circle on a dais, and in front of them sat two clerks of the court. The place for the accused and the witnesses was at the center. Jewish court procedure did not employ a prosecutor. His part was taken by the witnesses for the prosecution, and the evidence of at least two of them had to agree.

The evidence of the first witness was declared invalid; we do not know what it was. Jesus was then accused of saying that he would destroy the temple which had been built by people and erect another in three days (Mark 14:56 — 59). This would certainly have been considered a serious accusation, as the position of the temple was already threatened by the increasing influence of the synagogues and by the opposition of certain sects, for instance, that at Qumran. But this evidence was also rejected. An attempt was then made to make Jesus admit that he was guilty. Caiaphas rose from his seat, and everyone with him. He went up to Jesus and screamed: "'Have you no answer to make? What is it that these men testify against you?'" (Mark 14:60).

Jesus made no answer. The trial seemed to have reached an impasse. But then Caiaphas asked the decisive question: "'Are you the Christ, the Son of the Blessed?'" (Mark 14:61). Until that moment Jesus had avoided referring to himself as the Messiah, so that no one should be misled into expecting political intervention from him. Now he solemnly declared: "'I am; and you will see the Son of man sitting at the right hand of Power, and coming with the clouds of heaven'" (Mark 14:62).

Not only did Jesus give an affirmative answer, but he also referred to his return in

"...he (Pilate) brought Jesus out and sat down on the judgment seat at a place called The Pavement"

(John 19:13)

The Lithostratos and the Chapel of the Condemnation (left) are modern but beneath them can be discerned the foundations of the ancient fortress of Pilate's time. In Caesarea, a stone (right) bearing Pontius Pilate's name was found.

193

One of the outstanding relics
of Herod's palace is the
tower of Phasael, named for
the king's brother.

order to prove his divine identity. The simple "I am" carries within it the echo of God's own way of revealing himself, for anyone who wishes to hear. As an indication that he was grieved and annoyed, Caiaphas tore his clothes, because this claim to the divine honor of being the Messiah was "blasphemy." None of those present realized the final, profound meaning of the mission of Jesus as the true Son of God. There was no need for further witnesses, they had all heard the "blasphemy." They agreed that Jesus deserved the death penalty. It was a request to be made to the procurator—it did not amount to an official verdict.

JESUS BEFORE PILATE

As was customary, the crowd went to the Pretorium, the splendid palace of Herod on the site of the ancient citadel, to which three massive towers still bear witness today. Pilate, who was familiar with Jewish customs, came out to meet them because if they were to enter they would be transgressing against the Passover laws. The very first words spoken reveal the tension between the Romans and the Jews:

"'What accusation do you bring against this man?' They answered, 'If he were not an evil-doer, we would not have handed him over.' Pilate said to them: 'Take him yourselves and judge him by your own law.' The Jews said to him, 'It is not lawful for us to put any man to death'" (John 18:29—31).

Then there followed the indictment: "'We found this man perverting our nation, and forbidding us to give tribute to Caesar, and saying that he himself is Christ a king'" (Luke 23:2).

The religious accusations against him, which were so decisive as far as the Jews were concerned, were not even mentioned. Instead Jesus was represented as one rebelling against the authority of the state, while the Jews claimed for themselves the role of protecting it. They made extreme accusations which were to some extent distortions of the truth. For instance, Jesus had never incited anyone to refuse to pay taxes. Pilate himself then interrogated Jesus: "'Are you the King of the Jews?'" (John 18:33).

To which Jesus answered: "'My kingship is not of this world.... You say that I am a king.

196

The palace of Herod, on the site of the old citadel, was most likely Pilate's Jerusalem residence. Remnants can still be seen near the Jaffa Gate in the western part of the Old City of Jerusalem.

For this I was born, and for this I have come into the world, to bear witness to the truth. Every one who is of the truth hears my voice'" (John 18:36 — 37).

Jesus and Pilate: two worlds, each with its own and different truth. The one is a prophet of the divine word on his own divine authority, the other a representative of the modern liberal philosophy of life. Pilate was not capable of understanding what Jesus said. But he was certain of one thing: the man was entirely harmless. "I find no crime in him."

And therefore he did not want to have anything to do with the trial and made several attempts to get rid of Jesus. By chance, Herod Antipas from Galilee was in the city for the celebrations. He was living near the Wailing Wall in a Maccabean palace; during the Byzantine period, the Church of the Holy Wisdom was built into this structure, perhaps to commemorate an hour of Good Friday. To get Herod's opinion, Pilate sent Jesus to him; this was also a friendly gesture by Pilate that relieved the tension between him and Herod Antipas. Jesus did not vouchsafe one single word to the sovereign of his province,

"So they took Jesus, and he went out, bearing his own cross..." *(John 19:17)*

Thousands of pilgrims from all over the world take part in the Good Friday Procession, retracing Christ's footsteps (left).
The Third Station (right) marks Jesus' first fall.

who had him dressed in a white cloak to make him appear ridiculous, then sent him back to Pilate (Luke 23:8 — 12). The Roman soldiers gave him a great welcome, dressed him in a purple robe, and put a crown of thorns on his head (John 19:2 — 5). As part of this trial, the common Middle Eastern custom of making fun of someone gains a special significance in that it enacts all that had previously been said. The mockery and the irony revealed what the people were thinking: the Jews made fun of Jesus as a prophet and the Romans as a king. Jesus now looked pitiable, and Pilate showed him to the people with the famous *"Ecce homo."* Instead of laughing the people responded with fanatic shouts of "Crucify him!" The procurator looked for another way out. At that time it was customary in Palestine to grant an amnesty on the Passover, and so Pilate offered to release Jesus. The crowd demanded from him instead the release of Barabbas, and when Pilate asked them: "'Then what shall I do with the man whom you call the King of the Jews?'" he was told again: "'Crucify him'" (Mark 15:13).

Annoyed, he answered: "'Take him your-

"...(there was) in the garden a new tomb where no one had ever been laid" (John 19:41)

The Church of the Holy Sepulchre is built on the traditional site of Christ's tomb.
The present Basilica was erected by the Crusaders on foundations going back to the time of the Emperor Constantine.

selves and crucify him, for I find no crime in him'" (John 19:6).

Then the Jews at last revealed the actual reason for their hostility: Jesus ought to die "'because he has made himself the Son of God'" (John 19:7). Jesus was interrogated a second time; at first he was silent and then he answered with a reference to Pilate's competence as a human being: "'You would have no power over me unless it had been given you from above'" (John 19:11). By this he meant from God. Pilate was confused by this appeal to his conscience.

Then the people cried, "'If you release this man, you are not Caesar's friend; every one who makes himself a king sets himself against Caesar'" (John 19:12).

Pilate gave in. He climbed onto the tribunal — it was about the sixth hour on the day before Passover — and passed sentence: "You will be crucified." This was the way the Romans usually put people to death, and thousands of Jews had already been killed in this manner. He made a demonstration of washing his hands, which is a gesture of innocence; but Pilate was a Roman judge and so inescapably had to bear the full responsibility for the verdict. The gesture was therefore ironical. There was much irony contained in the part of the trial which took place before Pilate. It focused wholly on Jesus alone, and people made fun of him, which made the tragedy even more profound and at the same time gave it a deeper meaning.

The site of these events was probably the Place Lithostratos, paved with colored stones. The traditional Lithostratos on the Via Dolorosa provides a fairly good example of what it must have looked like. The design of pavements is not much subject to fashion, and although it dates from a later age it shows the old techniques still in use.

At the moment at which sentence was passed on him, Jesus stood alone and deserted. The enemies of Jesus and even Barabbas had their firm supporters. Only Jesus — to whom all men were brothers — was on his own; it is a most moving picture when seen against the environment from which he came. His disciples had become afraid and fled in all directions. In Gethsemane, Peter at least showed some courage and drew his sword; although

"And when they came to the place which is called The Skull (Calvary), there they crucified him..." *(Luke 23:33)*

The accepted Holy Sepulchre (left) is an ancient Jewish tomb but it has been enclosed in a modern chapel with a distinctive facade, marble pillars and columns. The lamps and candlesticks belong to the various Christian communities who worship here. On Calvary, the golden mosaic of the Latin Chapel (below) represents the scene of the Crucifixion (eleventh station). The altar on the left, tended by the Greek Orthodox, marks the place where Jesus' cross was fixed (twelfth station). Between the stations stands the Latin altar of "Stabat Mater" (thirteenth station).

Various communities worship in the
Basilica of the Holy Sepulchre.
Among them are the
Armenians whose colorful service
in the church is pictured.

The Garden Tomb (below) is outside the walls of the old city of Jerusalem. Some Protestants view the Garden Tomb as the actual burial place of Jesus. The inner chamber of the Garden Tomb (right).

later he betrayed his Lord. We are not told anything about the others: only one of them becomes prominent: Judas, seized by remorse, returned the money — which was later used to buy a cemetery for strangers — and hung himself.

THE CRUCIFIXION

The sentence was executed immediately. Jesus was scourged: he was bound naked to a pillar and whipped by soldiers until he was covered with blood and he collapsed. This moving scene must also be seen in its setting; such cruelty toward prisoners still occasionally occurs in the Middle East. Jesus had to drain the bitter cup of defeat to the dregs. Then he and two robbers were led by those detailed to execute them to the place of execution. On the way there he carried the crossbeam of his cross; the upright post had already been driven into place.

There is a historic foundation for the fourteen Stations of the Cross recognized by the Christian religion, with the exception of Veronica, which is legendary. When they reached the gate of the city, Jesus was exhaust-

ed and Simon of Cyrene, a farmer returning home from the fields to prepare his Passover, was ordered to help him carry the cross. Women lined the route; according to an old custom they were preparing an aromatic wine which would ease the pain. When it later was offered to Jesus he rejected it, because he wished to remain fully conscious while he was draining the cup of suffering. These women are a symbol of true humanity, illuminating the surrounding darkness. Golgotha, the place of execution, derives its name — meaning skull — from the shape of a rock there. Jesus was made to lie on the ground with outstretched arms, to be nailed to the cross. Probably pegs were driven through the wrists before he was raised onto the post, and afterward the feet were fastened. To prevent the body from tearing under its own weight, it was propped up between the legs and beneath the feet; the early Fathers say that it was as if he were sitting on a throne. Above his head, a board was fastened bearing in Aramaic, Latin, and Greek script the words: *Jesus of Nazareth the King of the Jews*. It was an ironic reference to the accusation that Jesus had claimed to be a king.

The two robbers were also crucified. There were many people present, though of course not Pilate. Authority was represented by a few soldiers. It was their traditional right to share the garments of the condemned among themselves. The tunic was without seams, woven in one piece; it probably resembled a tallith, the Jewish prayer shawl. As was his official duty, Caiaphas was waiting for Jesus to make a confession so that he might absolve him, but he waited in vain and eventually left to attend the divine service for Passover.

Mockery and irony permeated the last hours of the Lord. The typical derisive exclamation "Aha" (Mark 15:29) was part of it, and so was the sponge full of vinegar, which was intended to stop him from losing consciousness until "'Elijah will come to take him down'" (Mark 15:36). So also was the reference by the chief priests to his messianic mission when they called him King of Israel: "'Let the Christ, the King of Israel, come down now from the cross, that we may see and believe'" (Mark 15:32).

During these dark hours, a few of his followers had come to him, above all the women, including his mother, and also his favorite disciple, John. Jesus asked John to look after his mother for him. He was showing a concern for his family which is typical of the Jews, who see God himself as the father of the fatherless and protector of widows (Psalm 68:5). That he turned first to his mother indicates the close relationship between children and their mothers that can be observed everywhere in the Middle East. Finally, the last words of the dying man had a special significance. According to a widely held belief, those who are standing on the threshold of death achieve insights not granted to them during their life on earth. These words are, so to speak, the legacy Jesus left to his followers, who therefore cherished them faithfully and passed them on. This explains why the last words of Jesus must be accorded a very special significance. There is the magnificent phrase spoken in forgiveness, but there are also the words indicating that he felt himself to have been entirely abandoned (Matthew 27:46). Yet at the moment when the lambs had been sacrificed and the pilgrims in the temple area were to begin the evening prayer, Jesus who had been cast out and abandoned, with a loud voice joined in to pray with them according to the holy commandment: "'Father, into thy hands I commit my spirit!'" (Luke 23:46).

He altered the words slightly, and the change he made is very illuminating. Instead of pronouncing the name of God he prayed to his father; in obedience to him he sacrificed himself for his people, to make peace between them. And then he died; it was about three o'clock in the afternoon.

THE BURIAL

Because of its concern for hygiene, Jewish law did not permit any corpse to remain on the cross overnight. So soldiers came with clubs to break Jesus' thighs but found that he was already dead. One of them drove a spear into his side — probably into his chest — and immediately there flowed blood and water (John 19:34), that is "blood even fluid" with regard to levitical cleanness of the Paschal Lamb; for blood which streams forth is clean and that which drips forth is unclean. According to Roman law, there was a dispensation for those executed for political reasons, which meant that they could be given an honorable burial and did not have to be interred in some outlying place; Joseph of Arimathea asked Pilate for the body, and he and Nicodemus carried out the burial. Adding some fragrant spices, they wrapped the body in clean linen sheets and placed it in a tomb cut out of the rock. The tomb, in a garden near the place of execution, belonged to Joseph. It consisted of an antechamber with benches, where the mourners could pray, and an inner chamber which could be sealed off with a large stone wheel. Joseph and Nicodemus, members of the Sanhedrin, were secret followers of Jesus, and their action of charity toward a fellowman was of the sort which rich Jews are commanded to perform

The Tomb in the Church of the Holy Sepulchre in Jerusalem may be accepted as genuine. In what is today the Syrian chapel, several Jewish rock tombs have been discovered, indicating the existence of a cemetery there, originally lying outside the walls but later included by the Romans within the area of the city. Under Constantine, much earth and many rocks were moved in order to level the site for the church. There was a firm tradi-

"were going to a village named Emmaus..." *(Luke 24:13)*

After his resurrection, Jesus appeared to two of his disciples in a village called Emmaus. One tradition sites it sixty stadia (each 606 feet) from Jerusalem. Excavations have shown that this was a large Roman-Byzantine center with a "Broadway" flanked by houses, wine and oil presses. The church pictured was built on the foundations of an old house, traditionally called the home of Cleophas, one of Christ's disciples who first saw him risen from the dead.

tion, accepted by Constantine, that this was the place of the tomb of Jesus. It is possible that the tomb was marked by stones, an old custom, still practiced today by Jews and Arabs.

THE EMPTY TOMB

It was evening, and everywhere there was a sabbath stillness. A few guards were near the tomb; otherwise no one was about. The disciples also strictly observed the sabbath. According to John, Mary Magdalene came to the tomb the next morning, that is on Sunday, saw that the stone had been rolled aside, and assumed that someone had been there to remove the body. She informed the disciples. Peter and John raced to the place and entered the chamber. They saw the linen cloths and, lying a little apart from them, a kerchief. It looked not as if someone had fled in haste but as if he had left at leisure. They confirmed that the tomb was empty, without at first comprehending what had happened, but they were amazed — and their amazement was followed by faith. Mary remained behind when the others left. She heard herself spoken

to but did not suspect anything unusual, believing at first that it was the gardener. Suddenly she became aware that it was *Rabboni,* the master. She hurried after the disciples and called to them: "I have seen the Lord" (John 20:18).

THE RESURRECTION

On the morning of Easter Sunday the tomb of Jesus was empty. This was an uncontestable fact, and his enemies did not deny it. They spread the rumor that the disciples had stolen the body in the course of the night, while the guards were sleeping (Matthew 28:11 — 15). But this was not the true explanation. God revealed the truth to the women through the mouth of an angel: "'Do not be amazed; you seek Jesus of Nazareth, who was crucified. He has risen, he is not here'" (Mark 16:6).

Similarly, Matthew 28:2 mentions an earthquake to indicate that something supernatural had happened there. The meaning of the empty tomb is made clear by the appearance of the Resurrected One. Paul provides us with a list of witnesses who saw the Lord (1 Corinthians 15:3 — 8). It is formulated almost like

a legal document. The teaching of the disciples is based upon the joyful tidings: "God raised him on the third day and made him manifest... to us who were chosen by God as witnesses" (Acts 10:40 — 41). Only those who have witnessed the resurrection can be apostles. These are not people prone to succumb to visions or hallucinations, but sober men who accept that their testimony may bring with it persecution and death. And so the resurrection became a fact taking its place in actual history. Only those whose minds are receptive to it are able to appreciate its true spiritual significance. As it says in the Gospel According to John: "He saw and believed" (20:8).

THE APPEARANCES OF JESUS

We will select only a few of the occasions on which the Lord appeared after his resurrection. First, he appeared to Mary from Magdala, a woman whom others looked down upon. It indicates that Christ was concerned for the poor and forsaken and especially for women. Then there is the charming story of the disciples from Emmaus, who are on their way home from Jerusalem and sadly discuss the events which have just taken place; they are joined by an unknown wayfarer. When night comes they invite him, in true Middle Eastern fashion, to remain with them as their guest. While they are sharing a meal he makes himself known to them (Luke 24:13 — 35). The small village of Qubeibeh commemorates this event. Numerous oil and wine presses by the side of a Roman-Byzantine road indicate that in ancient times there was some sort of agricultural community there. Whether this was the actual place or not, the setting is the same. The disciples worked there; they are no dreamers but sober business people, who have to contend with the hard facts of life but at the same time have an open mind on questions of religion and the meaning of the religious existence.

On another occasion, as the disciples were sitting together, Jesus suddenly joined them. Nobody knew where he had come from, but they saw him as a real live person and, like the doubting Thomas, touched his stigmata. They were allowed to offer him something to eat, and they realized with amazement: he was a real person and not a phantom (Luke 24:36).

212

The resurrection of Jesus differed from that of, for instance, Lazarus. He came from another world. Mary was not allowed to touch him; he passed through locked doors; walls did not seem to exist for him. Nevertheless, he returned to the reality in which his disciples were living. They could not understand it; but they believed that it was true and bore witness to what they had seen and heard. Certainly, those who lacked insight would only have seen a gardener, a wayfarer, a stranger, and would have made nothing of it. And so it would have been useless if he had appeared before Caiaphas or Pilate.

All these occasions made people realize and believe in the resurrection. They were, at the same time, a proclamation and a mission. This became apparent by the Sea of Galilee, near Tabgha, where the river joins the lake and attracts shoals of fishes. One night Peter and others had gone fishing and not caught anything. They were returning in a bad humor when a stranger called to them from the shore to cast out their nets once more. They followed his advice and caught such a vast number of fish that they could hardly lift their nets on

Tradition holds that Christ, risen from the dead, had breakfast with his disciples. The place is traditionally sited in Tabgha Bay, now enclosed within the Church of the Primacy (right), where a rock (left) is shown as "Mensa Christi" ("Christ's Table"). Here also Peter was appointed to the leadership (primacy) of all other disciples of Christ with the words, "Feed my lambs . . . Feed my sheep."

...Feed my lambs... Tend my sheep... Feed my sheep'''
(John 21:15–17)

board. They recognized the stranger as the Lord, who was waiting. According to pious tradition, he prepared a meal for them on a rock that is still pointed out today. And this was the place and the occasion when Christ said to Peter: "'Feed my lambs... tend my sheep... feed my sheep'" (John 21:15—17).

The threefold repetition was the officially recognized way of making the transfer legal, first of all to Peter, but later also to those who came after him. Peter is both the rock and the good shepherd who must provide for his flock. It was probably the region in which Jesus once preached the Beatitudes, from which he now sent his disciples to preach the joyful tidings: "'Go therefore and make disciples of all nations, baptizing them in the name of the Father and of the Son and of the Holy Spirit, teaching them to observe all that I have commanded you; and lo, I am with you always, to the close of the age'" (Matthew 28:19—20).

His life on earth Jesus had dedicated above all to his own people; now, as he took leave of his disciples, he sent them out into the whole world. This is the framework in which we must see the coming of the Holy Spirit to the dis-ciples together with the authority to forgive and to retain sins (John 20:21—23).

THE ASCENSION

After his resurrection, Jesus remained with his disciples for forty days, in order to instruct them more thoroughly in the mysteries of the kingdom of God. "Then he led them out as far as Bethany, and lifting up his hands he blessed them. While he blessed them, he parted from them" (Luke 24:50—51).

Jesus was alone with his followers and left them to return to his divine glory. The short account by Luke does not contain any imaginative touches; he only reported the facts, without wishing to interpret the mystery. On the Mount of Olives there is a grotto which has been venerated as a place where Jesus taught his disciples; since the time of the Crusaders this is believed to have been the site where the Lord's Prayer originated. This is why the cloister bears the text of this prayer in various languages on more than fifty majolica tablets. The Emperor Constantine caused a basilica to be erected above this grotto and named it Eleona, as the Lord is said to have, at the close

216

of his ministry, ascended from there to heaven. But in the fourth century, an actual Church of the Ascension was erected opposite the basilica of Eleona. Originally it consisted of an open courtyard surrounded by columns, thus symbolizing the ascension in its structure; later the Moslems turned it into an enclosed mosque. According to Paulus of Nola (about A.D. 400), the ground there was made holy by the divine footprints, so that it was neither covered nor firmed down. Even today, the faithful venerate these last traces of the Lord before he left this world.

For some time after his resurrection, Jesus appeared to his disciples. Finally, he led the eleven apostles to the top of the Mount of Olives, gave his final instructions and ascended into heaven before their eyes. In Byzantine times, the Church of the Ascension was Jerusalem's great eastern landmark: a gleaming cross by day, a glowing lantern by night. Its only reminder now is a small mosque inside which, to the left, a legendary footprint left by the ascending Christ is shown.

"he blessed them, he parted from them... he was lifted up, and a cloud took him out of their sight"

(Luke 24:51; Acts 1:9)

HISTORICAL STUDY OF THE LIFE OF JESUS

Amiot, F., *Vie de Notre-Seigneur Jésus-Christ* (Paris, 1958).

Bauer, Walter, *Das Leben Jesus im Zeitalter der Neutestamentlichen Apokryphen* (Darmstadt: Wissenschaftliche Buchgesellschaft, 1967).

Ben-Chorin, Sch., *Jesus, Bruder Jesus* (München, 1967).

Benoit, P., *Passion and Resurrection of Jesus Christ* (London, 1969).

Bishop, J., *The Day Christ Died* (New York: Harper, 1957).

Blinzler, J., *The Trial of Jesus* (Cork, 1959).

Bornkamm, G., *Jesus of Nazareth* (New York, 1960).

Braun, F.-M., *Jésus, Histoire et Critique* (Paris, 1947.

Congar, Y., *Jesus Christ.* (New York: Herder, 1966).

Daniel-Rops, *Jesus in His Time.* (London: Eyre and Spottiswoode; Burns and Oates, 1956).

De Grandmaison, L., *Jésus-Christ. Sa personne, son message, ses preuves.* 2 vols. (Paris, 1929). English translation, 3 vols.

Flusser, D., *Jesus,* Hamburg, 1968.

Goodier, Alban, *The Passion and Death of Our Lord Jesus Christ* (New York: Kennedy; 9th printing, 1962).

Grant, Robert M., *The Earliest Lives of Jesus* (New York: Harper, 1961).

Guardini, Romano, *The Lord* (London: Longmans, 1960).

Hoffmann, J.G.K., *Les vies de Jésus et le Jésus de l'histoire* (Paris, 1947).

Kopp, C., *The Holy Places of the Gospel* (New York, 1962).

Kroll, G., *Auf den Spuren Jesu* (Leipzig, 1966).

Lagrange, M.-J., *L'Evangile de Jésus Christ* (Paris, 1928). English translation: *The Gospel of Jesus Christ.* 2 vols.

Lebreton, J., *Jésus-Christ* (Paris, 1931). English translation reprinted in 1957.

Leon-Dufour, X., *The Gospel and the Jesus of History* (New York, 1968).

Morton, H.V., *In the Steps of the Master* (London, 1937).

Pax. E., *Palästinensische Volkskunde im Spiegel der Kindheitsgeschichten* (Bibel und Leben 9), Düsseldorf, 1968.

Prat, F., *Jésus-Christ* (Paris, 1933).

Reatz, A., *Jesus Christus, sein Leben, seine Leben, seine Lehre und sein Werk* (2ed., Freiburg im Br., 1925).

Riciotti, G., *Vita di Gesù Cristo* (1941).

Schuerer, E., *A History of the Jewish People in the Time of Christ* (New York).

Schweitzer, A., *Geschichte der Leben Jesu-Forschung.* 6ed. (Tübingen, 1951).

Stauffer, E., *Jesus and His History* (New York, 1959).

Taylor, V., *The Life and Ministry of Jesus* (New York, 1955).

INDIVIDUAL SITES WITH GOSPEL REFERENCES

Bushell, G., *Churches of the Holy Land* (New York: Funk and Wagnalls, 1969).

Kopp, Clemens, *The Holy Places of the Gospels* (London: Nelson, 1963).

Pearlman, M. — Yannai, Y., *Historical Sites in Israel* (Massadah–P.E.C. Press, Tel Aviv, 1964).

TABOR

Sbrissa, O., "E forse il piu geniale e felice monumento cattolico di tutto l'Oriente," in *La Terra Santa* 30:10 (Ottob., 1954) 305–310.

JERUSALEM AREA

Aline, Soeur Marie, *La Forteresse Antonia à Jérusalem et la question du Prétoire* (Jerusalem, 1955).

Andres, P., "Historia y arqueologia en el Sto. Sepulcro," in *Tierra Santa* 40:433–444 (Mar.-Abr., 1965) 274–278.

Bagatti, B., "Autenticità del S.S.mo Sepolcro," in *La Terra Santa* 38:12 (Dic., 1962) 299–302.

Bagatti, B., "La Chiesa Madre del Sion," in *S. Giacomo il Minore.* (Jerusalem: Franciscan Press, 1962).

Bagatti, B., "Una pagina inedita della Chiesa primitiva di Palestina," in *La Terra Santa* 36:8–9 (Agost.-Sett., 1960) 230–236.

Benoit, P., "Prétoire, Lithostroton et Gabbatha," in *Revue Biblique* 59 (1952) 531–550.

Corbo, V., "Il Rinnovato Santuario di Betfage," in *La Terra Santa* 31:11 (Nov., 1955) 338–341.

Corbo, V., "'Dominus Flevit.' Il nuovo Santuario costruito sulle pendici dell' Oliveto," in *La Terra Santa* 33:8–9 (Agost.-Sett., 1957) 246–249.

Hoenig, S.B., *The Great Sanhedrin* (Philadelphia,

(1953).

Jeremias, J., *Jerusalem zur Zeit Jesu* (Göttingen, 1962).

Mancini, I., "Adam sous le Calvaire," in *La Terre Sainte* 1965:11–12 (Nov.–Cec.) 274–278.

Parrot, A., *Temple de Jérusalem* (Neuchatel-Paris, 1954).

Parrot, A., *Golgotha et Saint Sépulcre* (Neuchatel-Paris, 1955).

Saller, S.J., *Excavations at Bethany* (1949–1953). (Jerusalem: Franciscan Press, 1957.)

Storme, A., *Bethany*. (Jerusalem: Franciscan Press, 1969.)

Storme, A., *Gethsemani*. (Jerusalem: Franciscan Press, 1970.)

Testa, E., "Le 'Grotte dei Misteri' giudeo-cristiani," in *Liber Annuus* XIV (1963–1964) 65–144.

Vincent, H.—Abel, F.M., *Jérusalem de l'Ancien Testament*. 2 vols. Paris, 1954–1956).

Vincent, H.—Abel, F.M., *Jérusalem Nouvelle*. 2 vols. (Paris, 1914–1926).

EMMAUS

Bagatti, B., *I Monumenti di Emmaus el-Qubeibeh e dei Dintorni* (Jerusalem: Franciscan Press, 1947).

Emmaus. Santuario della Manifestazione in Fractione Panis (Jerusalem: Franciscan Press, 1953).

ASCENSION

Benoit, P., "L'Ascension," in *Revue Biblique* 56 (1949).

Corbo, V., "Scavo archeologico a ridosso della basilica dell' Ascensione," in *La Terra Santa* 37:1 (Gen., 1961) 31–32.

Corbo, V., *Ricerche Archeologiche al Monte degli Oliveti*. (Jerusalem: Franciscan Press, 1965).

NAZARETH

Bagatti, B., *Excavations in Nazareth*. (Jerusalem: Franciscan Press, 1969).

Olivan, A., "Nazareth, Son Sanctuaire, Sa Fontaine," in *La Terre Sainte* (Jerusalem: Franciscan Press) 7 (Aout–Septembre 1961, pp. 201–206.

Stiassny, M.J., *Nazareth* (G.A. The Jerusalem Publishing House, Jerusalem 1969).

EIN KAREM

Bagatti, B., *Il Santuario della Visitazione* (Jerusalem: Franciscan Press, 1948).

Cullmann, O., *Les Sacrements dans l'Evangile Johannique* (Paris, 1951).

Kraeling, C.H., *John the Baptist* (New York–London, 1951).

Saller, S.J., *Discoveries at St. John's 'Ain Karim* (Jerusalem: Franciscan Press, 1941–2).

BETHLEHEM

Abel, F.-M., *Bethléem* (Paris, 1914).

Bagatti, B., *Gli antichi edifici di Betlemme* (Jerusalem: Franciscan Press, 1952).

Corbo, V., *Gli Scavi di Kh. Siyar el-Ghanam (Campo dei Pastori) e i Monasteri dei Dintorni* (Jerusalem: Franciscan Press, 1955).

Hamilton, R.W., "Excavations in the Atrium of the Church of the Nativity," in *The Quarterly of the Department of Antiquities in Palestine* 3 (1934) 1–8.

Lugans, G., "Grotes de Bethléem," in *La Terre Sainte* 1964:12 (Dec.) 317–323.

Olivan, A., "Ancora una Grota col sorriso della Maternità divina," in *La Terra Santa* 30:7 (Lugl., 1954), 197–203.

T.B., "Il nuovo Santuario 'S.S. Angelorum ad Pastores'" in *La Terra Santa* 31:2 (Feb., 1954), 42–51.

CANA

Kopp, Clemens, *Das Kana des Evangeliums* (Cologne, 1940).

Loffreda, S., "Cana. Recenti scoperte," in *La Terra Santa* 45:11 (Nov., 1969) 346–350.

Mancini, I., "Novità su Cana evangelica," in *La Terra Santa* 42:7–8 (Luglio–Agosto, 1966) 205–210.

Wilmes, G., "Cana, Santuario del Primo Miracolo," in *La Terra Santa* 41:2 (Feb., 1965) 42–45.

CAPERNAUM

Bagatti, B., *La Capella sul Monte delle Beatitudini* (Rome, 1937).

Concetti, G., "Cafarnao. Nuovi scavi e scoperte," in *La Terra Santa* 46:1–2 (Gen.–Feb., 1970) 3–7.

Corbo, V.—Loffreda, S., *New Memoirs of Saint Peter by the Sea of Galilee*. (Jerusalem: Franciscan Press, 1969.)

Guerra, A., "Il Lago del Primato," in *La Terra Santa* 41:7–8 (Luglio–Agosto, 1965) 203–209.

McCowan, C., "The Problem of the site of Bethsaida," in *Journal of the Palestine Oriental Society* 10 (1930) 32–58.

TERRA HUS.

Gamela
Cedar

GERASAEORUM

RACHONITIS

Ga Zwethanita

REGIO

Astaroth REGIO

Labis

Galaad

Rara

Carnay Iaboc

Fabis

Tubbin Massha

Casshor Gadera

Pinel Araboth Mons Betho

Iaboc torrens

Succoth

Iordanis fluuius

Corazaim
Iuliada

Adama
Lekum

Caldes

Shion

Ierceon

Capharn aum

Ephraim

Iordanis fluuius

Illustris vallis

Pella
Pella

Araboth

Dimidia Tribus Manasses

Salim

Enon

Mare Galilææ vel
Tiberiadis quod
et Stagnũ Gene-
zareth

Tarichea
Ieſſerkin

Magdalum

Debir

Dion

Amuaus toparchia

Amuaus

Mageth

Bezeloch

Acraba
Toparc hia

Acra

Balim tena

Jordanis partius

Tiberias

Neptalim

Hamdu Hinassach

Asnoth

vel Hesron
Antiopia

Chartan

Harozeth

Horma

Sidimzer

Bethleem

Cabul

Zephet

Genezareth

Gabaroth

Abel

Betho
cha

Betmanu
sha

Amathuntha

Hippon

Belvoir

Bethsan
Scythopolis

Gruna bar

Therme

Itaburus mons

Arbel

Thebes

Thenae

Enaberis

Magnus camp us Sa

Israel, Gerinum.

marie

Ferra torrens

Thersi

Therpi

Forda

Geba

LI
SUPERIOR SEU
GENTI
UM L

Dotham Fu.

Bersaida Iulias

Fatapata

S. Elkofi

Abdon

Kanathou

Dotham

Abelna

Galara

Bethulia

Belina

Thabor mons

Chelma

Endor

Rubavia

Hanoth Flu

Naim

Bellifort

A.

Kision

S A

Semeron M.

Tribus Aser

Amma

Cikessa

Amead

Naason

Selama

Masal

Tribus Zabu
lon

Rama

Aeschim

Buria

HEVAEI

Adremmŏ
Faba

Darabitta

Gergesei

Genim
Gehoru

Sebaste Santaria

M

For San

Dan

Montfort

Hossa

Vallis Ieph
thael

Charta

Zabulon

PHOE NI

Indi

Fons aquarum
viventium

Berthdagon

GALILEA

Sephor

Nazareth

Meshra

Faknoam

INFERIOR

Pheresæ

Gahaa
Hippon

Aphee

Abee

Esdrolm

Anat.

Bethsemes

Mons Bothe

TRI Ibus

Narbatha

Assur

S. Georgy

Amead

Soron vel
S. Lamperti

Ptolemais
Acon

Abdon CIA

Cana Galilæe

Sihor

Sepulchrum
Memnonis

Chison torrens

Narbathæ toparch ia

Cain

M. Carmelus

Arethasa

Subimbre

Montes Megidon

Isach ar

Delus torrens

Castrum Pere
grinorum, olim
Dora

Cæsarea
Palæstinæ

Campus

Mare Syriacum

D I T E R

E I

R A S